REUNION

WITH

SOURCE

Prophecies and Understandings
Concerning the Past and Future
of Humanity and the Earth

By Cazekiel

Received through James Gilliland

Copyright © 2016, 1995 by James Gilliland
ISBN 978-1-329-84445-2
Originally Published as Becoming Gods
First Edition ISBN 0-926524-34-8
Published by Wild Flower Press 1995
Second Edition ISBN 0-9658713-1-2
Published by Self-Mastery Earth Institute 1998
Third Edition ISBN 978-0-9658713-2-7
Published by Self-Mastery Earth Institute 2001
Third Printing August 2007
Fourth Edition 2016 Published by Eceti

Cover Photo: Mother Mary's apperance at the
Bridgehouse Sanctuary, photo by Mona Leigh Turner

ECETI
Phone: (509) 395-2092
Email: ecetireservations@gmail.com
YouTube: ECETI Stargate Official YouTube Channel
Website: www.eceti.org

And God created man in His own image, in the image of God
He created him: male and female He created them.
Genesis 1:27

Has it not been written in our Law, "I said you are gods."
John 10:34

That they all may be one, as thou, Father art in me, and I in
thee, that they also may be one in us. John 17:21

Know ye not that ye are the Temple of God and the spirit of
God dwelleth in you? Corinthians 3:16

Table of Contents

In Appreciation

My greatest appreciation is to the Father Mother God principle that gave me life; my parents for providing a vehicle to experience life upon this plane and the environment for growth; the Beautiful Many Angelic and Ascended Masters; and Cazekiel, the main author of this book. I wish to give special thanks to my self-mastery student/ teachers who supported these simple, yet outrageous, teachings, and all those who felt and acknowledged the love, wisdom and joy, making it possible for me to continue, often against all odds.

I desire to express my deepest admiration and appreciation to Patricia and Carolyn for their assistance, their courage, their insight and their open minds and loving hearts, which made the publishing of this book possible.

I also wish to thank those who disbelieved, challenged and tested these teachings, thus building my own character, conviction and steadfastness. I bless and honor their truth.

Godspeed,
James

Preface

The information in this book is true. It transcends religious dogma, scientific dogma, social consciousness, and will manifest as factual in the days to come. To some it will be unbelievable, to others it will resound as truth in their hearts and empower them to expand into, own, and remember their divine origin. You are all eternal beings.

You are loving, joyous, wise and powerful manifesting Gods and Goddesses. You have experienced many lives, on many planes and many dimensions. You have ancestors in the stars as well. This book is a beginning and a foundation to assist the radical few who have the courage and desire to start an outrageous journey toward a reunion with source-an interdimensional voyage into omnipresence.

Introduction

I am Cazekiel. I was better known to humanity as Ezekiel of the past. I am part of an unseen brotherhood that loves you greatly. I and many other authors of the past are coming forward at this time to bring to humanity a new understanding of God and the Universe. It is our desire to clear up the misperceptions and wrong conclusions from past experience concerning the nature of God, and lay to rest the fictitious, jealous, wrathful God, as well as the codes and the doctrines created to appease this image.

Humanity has come to a point in evolution where it must replace its graven images in favor of an omnipresent, omnipotent, omniscient God of pure unconditional love and joy. It is imperative that each individual be honored as a unique expression of the omnipresent God, and humanity must also behave as if the God in all life matters.

Fear and unworthiness are the barriers that separate humans from God. They are the by-products of ignorance. You cannot love God with all your heart if fear is present and if you have judged yourself to be unworthy. If you have accepted the judgments of others or their images, codes and doctrines, you will never see the face of God. It takes a fearless, joyous, unconditionally loving entity to become one with God, and it is all done within self. It is an inward journey. The temple is within. God is within, and only when humans have overcome their fear, unworthiness and ignorance will they be successful in reuniting with the God within. It is the purpose of these teachings to reveal the true origin of humanity, the true nature of God, and to clear any misperceptions that led to the wrong conclusions from past experience. They are also given to assist humanity to understand, assimilate and flow with the higher consciousness and energy that is cyclically, exponentially and vibrationally lifting and healing the Earth with all its inhabitants.

This is done in service to a God of pure, unconditional love and joy in the hope that you will be one as we are one. Reunion with Source is a journey into the realization of what you already are, always have been, and always will be. No matter how hard you try, you cannot separate yourself from Omnipresence. You can only live the illusion. Let the journey begin ....

Quotes from Meister Eckhart, mystical Christian theologian of the Middle Ages:

If I am to know God directly
I must become completely God, and God I,
so that this God and I become one.

As pear seeds produce pears and nut seeds
produce nut trees, God seeds produce Gods.

I became Man for you.
If you do not become God for me,
you do me wrong.
(Contemplating what God might say to Man.)

1

In the Beginning...

Creation

In the beginning was consciousness. Thought preceded the word. Consciousness, or thought, is the omniscient, omnipresent and omnipotent mind of God. Thought is the cause and form is the effect. All that is began first as thought, which is the highest vibration. Thought vibrations are lowered into light, lowered again into energy and lowered once more to create mass. Consciousness and energy are the nature of reality.

God, the original consciousness or thought, bent inward and contemplated self. There was a tremendous explosion of light and born were the children of light. The children of light who are you-were born of the first cause, or consciousness, from which nothing was withheld. The love, joy, power and wisdom of God, along with the creative drive, was given to each and every one of you evenly and unconditionally.

The children of light, Gods, or the Elohim, which is plural for God, went out into the universe endowed with the creative consciousness of God. They took thought and lowered it into light. Their first creations were the suns which are, in their most unlimited understanding, thought lowered one degree. Out of the suns were born planets, which were swirling bands of energy thrown out into cradle orbits around the suns. Due to the nature of gravity, which in truth is a push by the other heavenly bodies, and centrifugal force, heavier elements were spun outward, eventually cooling and solidifying to create the outer crust. The center remained a hot fiery sun.

Through time, the outer crust continued to cool and solidify. The core also condensed and cooled. Every planet within the universe is hollow and has a central sun. It was once factual that the Earth was flat. A few outrageous individuals set out to prove it was round despite violent resistance from the clergy and the prominent scientists of the time. Nonetheless the Earth is round. Yet, to be more accurate, it is more like a flattened sphere bulging at the seams.

Your scientists are watching planets form in distant galaxies. Some of them are at different stages of development and have not yet solidified in their outer crust. There are great cracks or fissures in the crust with light shooting out of them. There are also existing planets (Mercury is one such planet) which have light shooting out both poles.

Scientists have tried, unsuccessfully, to explain away this phenomenon. Lord knows, they cannot rewrite the astronomy books, lose their credibility, and give up their theories. Admiral Byrd discovered this in his journey to the North Pole. It is written within your Indian and Nordic lore. Your government is very aware of this, and it will be written again and accepted as reality due to events that are soon to unfold in your very near future. It is imperative that this understanding is given, risking the possibility of losing a few of you who have chosen to rely on those who believe the center of the Earth is molten rock. Ask them if they have ever been there. What is the source of the winds coming out of what they call breathing holes, which seem to go to unfathomable depths, and how do they explain what is obvious when looking at the formation of planets in distant galaxies? Now that we have gotten through the shock of a hollow Earth, let us continue.

As the crust cooled, there was a great cloud cover around the Earth. The waters fell and the land soon became suitable for life, and the cell was introduced along with the genetic codes to manifest the dreams of the Elohim. Thought was impressed into the cells, creating the genes. Genes, "the physical manifestation of thought," began to guide the cells to manifest the images of the Elohim. The birds, the fishes, the flora and even your body are all manifestations of the dreams and images of the Elohim, "the Gods."

It all began with thought. Each manifestation allowed one to be built upon the other. The mineral kingdom supplied the platform for the plant kingdom, and the plant kingdom made it possible for the herbivores. Herbivores became food for the carnivores, eventually creating the balance of life.

Humans were later created to provide a vehicle for the Elohim to walk among their creations, smell the flowers, walk upon the lush green carpets of moss and grass, and experience the world of form. They could not do this in their light bodies, for a light body-though it can see and feel-lacks the vehicle and the five senses to truly experience mass. Their light bodies flowed through mass.

The first vehicles, "bodies," were androgynous. They all looked the same and were neither male nor female. This became very confusing, for they never knew who was who, and they did not have the means to reproduce themselves. They were eventually recalled.

The second attempt was more successful, for they created two different types of bodies-male and female. This provided vehicles that would perpetuate themselves and created the vehicles necessary to house the Gods who, at this point, were very eager to walk upon the Earth.

"So God created man in his own image, in the image of God he created him; male and female he created them." (Genesis 1:27)

At this point in time, the Gods could come and go at will, and they did. In their zest for creativity, the images they projected into the first cells consisted of animals that were both herbivores and carnivores. They created the herbivores to balance the plant kingdom, and the carnivores to balance the herbivores. The Elohim had no understanding of fear, pain or death, for these feelings were not of their kingdom. The Elohim were of spirit. The options of fear, pain and death were only available to them when they entered the body.

This was the beginning of limitation, for the baser attitudes and emotions of pain and fear lowered the vibration of the Elohim. Many became entrapped within the bodies. Because of their altered, fearful state, they were unable to leave the body and return to the higher state of consciousness. Since the beginning of fear, humans have been very creative with lower vibrational thought and have considerably lowered their original vibration, or consciousness. Through the years, in their struggles to survive, humanity has been subject to their environment, rather than lord over their environment. They are now at a point in evolution where survival does not weigh so heavily upon their minds. It was the struggle to survive and the fear of pain and death that began the journey into limitation. The original sin or fall of man was not a sin, but a choice to walk among and experience his own creation. Those who chose to enter the body equipped with the five senses and engage matter are the greater for it. Wisdom equates power, and a treasure house of wisdom has been gained over the many incarnations. Those who choose can now take the time to gaze at the stars, contemplate their origin as co-creators born of the original light, and start to awaken and remember, thus beginning the journey home.

The Soul and Multilevel Being

As we have seen, after the first division and the creation of the suns, the planets and the mineral, plant and animal kingdoms, the Elohim (the Gods) also created the vehicles to walk among their creations. The vehicles (bodies) were created in the same image and likeness of the Gods, and in order to inhabit the bodies, they again lowered their vibrations and created the Soul.

The soul is an aspect of the God that created it. It is designed to govern the body and to record all that the body experiences. It was also equipped to make adjustments to the body, adapt it to different environments, and evolve the body to better suit the God that inhabited it. It is part of a vibrational continuum. Humanity is the chosen vehicle of the Gods that created the universe. It is written that "Ye are Gods and the spirit of God dwells within you." This is indeed a fact. Within you resides a great God. It is buried under layers of fear, unworthiness and wrong conclusions from past experience. The soul, which once was a shining example and counterpart of a great God, through time has been altered greatly by false identification with lower vibrational attitudes and emotions. Your true identity is neither the fear nor the unworthiness. You are not the wrong conclusions from past experience. You are not what you have been told by your parents, society or the holy men who keep you in darkness and subservience. You are Gods. You forgot now, didn't you?

It was Paul who said, "We have bodies celestial and bodies terrestrial"-another example of this understanding. As one expands in consciousness, one expands upward and outward along a vibrational continuum consisting of many levels. This process has been called many things, and the levels have been given many names. Some call it "contacting the higher self," "the holy spirit" or just plain "enlightenment." As one expands along this continuum, they experience higher, more unlimited states of consciousness. Thought has a vibration, and the most unlimited thoughts are pure, unconditional love and joy. It is no wonder that you experience more love, joy and sometimes ecstasy in expanded states of consciousness. This is also where genius originates. There are meditations and initiations that will help you enter states of higher consciousness.

Those who have made conscious contact with higher planes and dimensions can assist you in your journey, yet this process must be done with integrity and in honor of each individual as a unique expression of God. It also must honor your divine right to free will and self determination. You all have your own unique purpose for being.

Will & Personality

Each and every one of you has free will. This freedom allows you the divine right of self determination. With this gift comes responsibility, for you are living in an action-reaction world, known as the plane of demonstration, where consciousness creates reality. You came to this plane called "Earth" to live a loving, joyous, abundant life with a strong reverence for life in all forms.

There are many levels of consciousness. The will determines which level each individual chooses to express from or to be his or her identity. It is wise to turn the will over to the highest level of consciousness. This understanding was given when Jesus said, "I of myself do nothing. The Father within me doeth the works." Another prayer is, "Not my will, but thine be done." (Luke 22:42) There is a danger to self and others when the will is placed in the hands of the personality or the intellect. Both are riddled with fear, unworthiness, anger, "againstness," greed and a whole host of baser attitudes and emotions.

The personality (or the intellect) can justify and defend almost any action or behavior. When you go beyond the personality, love is the manifesting force behind all action-love of God, love of humanity, love of nature. The vast majority of governing bodies upon the Earth are run by personalities and intellects. Even most of your religious organizations are run by intellectual understandings and personalities. If the will were given over to the higher aspects of self, you would not have the problems of today's society. What you would have is Eden.

There is a mind known as divine mind, and its reasoning is divine reasoning. It is within each and every one of you. It is beyond the personality, and it is who you truly are. Your personality is just one of many garments. Your intellectual understanding is created by parents, society and the environment.

When the soul or higher levels of self are governing your life, all action will be based upon love and will be in the highest and best good of humanity and nature. Your soul is God, and God is love. If you want to know what level your will is operating on, look at your life. If you want to know the level of will of those who govern you, look at your society and the world in which you live. It is quite obvious that the will must rise to a higher level.

The Universe

The universe, or "One Verse," is like a grand puzzle. It is all coming together, and it is all God. There is nothing separate from omnipresence. To believe Creation began and ended with the Earth is to believe in error. You are all remnants of previous colonies and civilizations that have risen and fallen due to various causes. Some have been natural causes, and some have been due to unbridled greed and the lust for power, along with technology advancing at a more rapid rate than spirituality. There is more to your story and the universe than you can imagine.

I would like to begin with an explanation of form, or body. The body is a physical adaptation to the environment. Just as there are many races upon your planet, there are also many races throughout the cosmos. There are many environments that differ greatly from the Earth. And, there are many adaptations to these environments. The spirits within these bodies are all born of the original light. Thus, you are all family.

We spoke earlier of the Elohim, "the Gods born of the original light." Not all of the Gods chose to incarnate or lower their vibration into a physical body. Many remained in spiritual bodies and are working in the unseen to remind their brethren, the forgotten Gods, of their heritage. They incarnate from time to time as avatars and masters, and live their lives as examples of the God within humans. Jesus, Buddha, Babaji, White Eagle, Mohammed, Mary and a whole host of other saints and sages have incarnated at various times in your history as examples of the original light. They all spoke of one God, one family and one law. That was the law of love. They spoke to the cultures they incarnated into through the use of symbols and forms they could understand. They are responsible for the universal truths found throughout all religions. They are the examples of unifying with the God within.

There are many mansions, and the Elohim were not limited to this plane, this dimension or this planet. They manifested other vehicles (bodies) on other planes, dimensions and planets, and each civilization is at a different stage in evolution. These civilizations also took different paths in their evolutionary processes. Some evolved mentally and are very technologically advanced, yet void of emotions. Some evolved body, mind and spirit, and their technology is a reflection of their spirituality. Others chose the body and its environment to be their evolutionary process and again, and many never left spirit. This understanding will cause many of you to categorize those civilizations in a hierarchical order, yet I must remind you that experience equates wisdom and wisdom equates power. Those who have ventured into all these planes and dimensions have a greater understanding of God and the universe because they have experienced more of God and the universe.

Many advanced civilizations have interacted with Earth. Each civilization acted according to its accepted customs and beliefs, which were quite different from each other. Some acknowledged the divinity and diversity of all life and humanity's divine right to free will and self-determination. They came to guide and assist humanity. They were compassionate, loving and understanding.

There were others who came to rule humanity and be worshipped. They were jealous, wrathful and merciless. Cities and villages were decimated for refusing to worship them as Gods or follow their rules and doctrines. This in itself is a major contribution to the division in beliefs concerning the nature of God. Is He wrathful? Peaceful? All loving? Merciful? Omnipresent or somewhere else in the ethers?

There have been those who see humanity as a lower form of life to experiment with. There are also civilizations that are of your same seed who are spiritually and technologically advanced and are assisting humanity in its evolutionary process. Those who have interacted negatively with humanity are being removed from this plane. The scars and images they have left behind are also now being addressed and healed.

The universe is as infinite as God is. Humanity is soon to become aware of, and come into alignment with, other planes and dimensions and civilized planets within those planes and dimensions. The Earth's destiny is to take its rightful place as a part of a federation of planets in cooperation with their loving brothers and sisters-seen and unseen. As always, there is more to the story.

The Healing & Destiny of Earth

There is a cosmic event occurring throughout the universe. It is a quantum leap, or shift, into the next phase. Earth and all of its inhabitants are being vibrationally lifted. Earth will eventually come into alignment and take its rightful place in a federation of planets interacting with the civilizations that reside upon them. This will include other planes and dimensions as well. The veils are being lifted, the clouds are dispersing, and humanity will soon come to realize it is not alone in the universe.

Jesus is presiding over this event, for he has earned the position due to his great love, compassion and service to humanity. The Earth is divided into four quadrants. There are four omnipresent masters presiding over each of the four quadrants under the direction of Jesus. They are known throughout the universe as Andromedans. To humanity, they are known as Archangels. Michael, Gabriel, Uriel, Raphael and a host of other Andromedans, along with legions, are part of this endeavor. The legions consist of other spiritually and technologically advanced civilizations. The people from the Pleiades, Orion and those based within the Earth (a book in itself) are all working together as part of this endeavor.

The pure unconditional love and joy of God is being channeled spiritually and technologically upon Earth, raising all that is of a lower frequency or vibration. All lower vibrational attitudes and emotions, their physical manifestations, and all wrong conclusions from past experience are in the process of being vibrationally lifted and healed. There has been a band of energy placed around the entire planet that is a great amplifier. It is creating polarities of fear and joy. People are choosing the polarity they desire to be the manifesting force behind creation. In other words, things are going to be a little chaotic for awhile. It is the sword before the peace. The destiny of Earth is to be a reflection of the loving, joyous Gods that reside upon her. This reflection is also to be an example of a civilization that loves God with all its heart, honors each individual as a unique expression of God, including self, and reverently cherishes the God in all life. This will give you an indicator as to where changes are necessary, the extreme of such changes, and what you can do to flow with these changes.

This lifting is occurring within the mental, emotional and physical bodies. The Earth body is also a part of this process, and she, too, is on the move in her healing and cleansing process. The collective consciousness, as well as the astral cloud surrounding the Earth (which contains lower vibrational discarnate spirits, negative thought forms and limiting mental concepts), is also in the process of being healed and lifted. There is no rock being left unturned. It is a gift. It would be wise not to resist it, but to flow with it and to make any necessary changes within yourself, your job and your environment. It is an answer to a prayer of billions, seen and unseen. It is cyclic in nature and exponential in its intensity.

Ancient Ships

This next understanding is going to be a shock to some of you, a grand "Aha!" and realization to others, and completely unthinkable and blasphemous to those who wish to remain entrenched in religious dogma.

The pillar clouds and pillars of fire that guided and caught up Moses and Elijah, and the bright cloud in which they returned, were a great ship. The parting of the Red Sea was caused by this ship, and the pillar cloud which was afire by night guiding the Israelites out of

Egypt, and which caused the Egyptian army to grow heavy and unable to proceed, was also a ship. The fire and thunder on the mountaintops with their phenomenal experiences were again encounters with these ships. The inspiration for your religions came from these ships. If one reads any sacred book, one will realize that a pillar cloud, a pillar of fire, a chariot of fire, or a viamana[1] are present.

Upon these ships reside what we refer to as "angels"-spiritually and technologically advanced beings. Peter, James and John witnessed Jesus ascend into a great ship where he was transfigured. Moses and Elijah were also upon this great ship. Those you know as archangels reside upon these ships, and they inspired the prophets. They were responsible for Mohammed meeting Gabriel, Buddha climbing the Great Wall, and several of what are known as immaculate conceptions.

This information is not to discredit Jesus or the prophets.

They were! It is not to deny the existence of God. God is! The purpose of this information is to give credibility and understanding to the past. There are beings that are unique, yet one with God. There are whole civilizations of them. There are other beings at different levels or understandings in their evolutionary process. Some are physical to this dimension, others are physical to their dimension only. There are those who have bodies that are composed of energy. There are also those who exist in bodies that consist of magnetized light. These are known as the archangels.

The next question many ask is, "What does an omnipresent being need with a ship?" Why do you have a washing machine or a gas stove? Surely you could wash your clothes by hand, boil water,. and cook your food on an open fire. Why do you have a house when surely you can live anywhere? You are mobile, you know.

The ships are for the sake of convenience. They are necessary to traverse time, distance and space and to engage matter. In some cases, they are purely for your sake. They are needed to take you somewhere. After all, we just can't leave you out in space and teach you at the same time. Many of your prophets, saints, sages and masters speak of being caught up, transfigured and returned, after which their missions began. There was a transference of powerful consciousness and energy that made it possible to accomplish their goals.

These ships and their angelic crew are here again, and they will make themselves known with signs and wonders on the Earth and in the sky. Their presence will be introduced gradually so as not to create mass hysteria and panic. They are not here to conquer you. Those who were here for their own selfish gain and desire to be worshipped are gone, never to return. These present ships and their inhabitants

[1] Tibetan word for 'fiery chariot.'

are not here to be worshipped, and they are not here to evacuate you from the Earth during the healing process. This would interfere in your evolution, for you learn from the reactions to your actions.

They are here, as before, to inspire peace, harmony and a clean, wholesome, balanced life in harmony with nature. They are also here to promote a God of pure, unconditional love and joy: a God that loves and cherishes all life because it is all life; a God that has chosen you as its temple: the one consciousness, that encompasses all consciousness, with which they are one. They are here to inspire and usher in a new world where love is the manifesting force behind all creation, and each individual is honored as a unique expression of God. They are here because you are ready to understand a greater reality beyond the superstitious ignorance of the past.

Popular questions asked by many are, "Why have they not contacted our government?" and "Why don't they land in Central Park?" Your government is very aware of them. Your government has the wreckage of a few ships, as well as the bodies of a few unfortunate aliens who died in various crashes. They also had a live alien for a while. They don't have the great ones, however. The Orion, Pleiadian and Andromedan ships have been nothing more than phantoms and intimidators. The question as to why they don't land in Central Park can best be answered by reminding you of a past event. A primitive spacecraft was sent into space some years ago. It was called Voyager. It had a message concerning the people of Earth. It said, "Welcome, we greet you in peace."

So humanity as a collective was saying that they want to unite with the rest of the universe and have contact. So a ship appeared. The Air Force was alerted. They sent their fighters to chase, capture or shoot down anything that was foreign to their own. If great beings went for a stroll in Central Park they would be worshipped as Gods, incarcerated by your government and probed, questioned and dissected by overzealous scientists.

If they left their ship, everyone would want a piece of it, including your government. The message in the Voyager should have said, "Welcome, we want your technology, your weaponry. Our government needs the target practice. If you land we will incarcerate you, hide you from the people and neither you nor your ship will be able to go home." You do not know whom you are dealing with. These ships have the capacity to vaporize a continent, turn it upside down and make it vanish in a moment. They could turn this planet into a cinder-end of planet. Your government has sent fighters to engage them, and they disappear into another dimension or cruise along at several thousand miles an hour, making right angle turns. They defy all your known laws of physics. This should be quite humbling, yet there are those who, in ignorance, continue to pursue them-not in peace, but with a desire to conquer them. How primitive! If you want to make contact with spiritually and technologically advanced beings, stop being so primitive!

Demand that your government establish a non-threatening policy. While you are at it, ask your government to reveal the monumental evidence and artifacts they have kept from you. More important, work on your own fear and "againstness." Create an opening and desire within self to have contact. They will know when you are ready. It may happen when you least expect it. It may be on a secluded country road, high in the mountains, in a vast and barren desert, or even in your own backyard. One day you will look up, and they will be just sitting there or moving quietly through the sky. They may come straight down from the heavens and split into four different directions, or they may just streak across the night sky at breakneck speed. Nonetheless, they are real.

Ground Crew

We, the Ascended Masters, have spoken of the celestial part of the planetary lifting. We would also like to address the terrestrial counterpart. There are many of you knowingly and unknowingly assisting in the lifting and healing of the Earth. Many are being used as vibrational bridges, anchoring the higher vibrations of love, joy, peace and unity upon the planet. From our perspective, they are seen as columns of light. Many are not aware of the source of this energy, yet they are aware of the nature of it. They are also aware of the benefits of choosing unconditional love and joy as the manifesting forces behind all creation.

The ground crew is as diverse as humanity. People in all walks of life are awakening to their true purpose for incarnating upon this plane. Deep within them is a voice telling them, "There is more. There is a higher purpose, another way of life, a more peaceful, loving, joyous, abundant way of life with a greater awareness." They are asking themselves, "I know I came here to do something very important. What did I come here to do? Why am I here anyway? This just isn't working. There must be more." They are the awakening ground crew.

Many are fully awakened. They are the pioneers. They are awakening others in their own unique way. This higher consciousness and energy is moving through a variety of administrations, organizations and individuals that have packaged and named it everything under the sun. The name of the organization is unimportant. It is the goals and intentions that are important. People are coming forward in all walks of life, awakening and remembering their true purpose for being. They are stepping out of confusion, healing wounds from their former incarnations or Earth sojourns, and stepping into their chosen destinies.

This awakening and remembering is fully supported and implemented in a divine plan, the magnitude of which is incomprehensible. You are not alone in this endeavor, neither above nor below. You are the seeds of forever. Now is the time to awaken to your purpose, to regain your self-authority and integrity, and to move forward in the healing and lifting of this plane.

The Seven Densities of God

To give you a greater picture of the universe, which is better understood as Uni(one) Verse(song), we wish to combine dimension with density. A common analogy everyone is familiar with and can understand is water. Water can change in vibration from ice to water to steam, yet it is still water. So it is with the seven densities of God. They are all different vibrations of the same essence. Let us say the mineral kingdom is first density, the plant and insect kingdom is second density, and the animal kingdom is third density. We will talk about these first three densities because this is what humanity, as a collective, is aware of and knowledgeably interacts with. We will later address the planes just beyond the third, known as the astral planes.

The mineral kingdom made it possible for the plant and insect kingdom, and they, in turn, made it possible for the animal kingdom. They are built one upon the other, support each other, and are interdependent upon each other. And they are all holy. There are higher forms of the animal kingdom within the third density that share an individual sense of self along with humanity. Yet, for the most part, they are instinctual and react to their environment, versus having the ability to make conscious intentional decisions to alter it. Each human consists of a third density body in which resides a unique, loving, joyous, free-willing God-a God that can consciously and intentionally interact with and alter the lower densities. If he or she were smart, these lower densities would be left to themselves.

This conscious interaction has throughout time, for the most part, been unaware of the delicate balance and necessity of all densities to support one another. Any interaction or alteration must take all levels into account, the consequences to one affect the whole. The better portion of humanity has chosen to identify with the body, the conscious mind and the five sensory inputs recorded by the body. This is a third density or three-dimensional identity. The third density is only aware of itself and the two lower densities or dimensions. It is a limited identity, for there are four more levels of which most of humankind is unaware.

There is a fourth, fifth, sixth and seventh density. The body is endowed with the ability to sense and raise its vibratory frequency to identify with and experience all seven densities, or dimensions, of God. All seven densities exist within you, and you have the ability to experience all seven densities of God through a divine system called "the chakras" or "the seven seals." That is why the Gods chose the vehicle of humanity to be their home.

So you thought you weren't holy? What you are is asleep. As a collective, you have been operating out of the first three chakras. The first is base survival, the second is sexual reproduction, and the third is power. Even these are often misdirected. The next density is love, and it corresponds with the fourth chakra. Humanity is in the process of being vibrationally lifted into the fourth density, which is love felt for all things, love of self, love of humanity, love of nature and love of God.

We have spoken of the fourth density or dimension where love is the manifesting force behind all creation. Love is a powerful force, or vibration; it heals and raises all lower vibrations. This is called the "quickening." It is also known as "amplification." The first, second and third densities will still exist. Love is what holds them together and all creation based upon love will continue. Only the baser creations will discontinue, along with the baser attitudes and emotions. This is when the lion will lie down with the lamb.

Those who are fourth density beings are not visible to the third. Though they have a body and a world that is physical to them, it is not physical to the third density. They are of a different frequency. As humanity is vibrationally lifted into the fourth density, other fourth dimension beings become more and more visible. This is already happening. These fourth density entities are spiritually and technologically advanced. They have ships that can traverse dimensions. These ships are also on the fifth, sixth and seventh densities. They are even on your third density. Whole books concerning your government's involvement with UFOs have already been written. Your government also has some of these ships, but they haven't yet figured out time.

Those on the fourth density can manifest within the third by lowering their vibratory frequency. All higher density beings can manifest in a lower density, but lower density beings are often not aware of, or consciously able, to raise their frequency to meet the higher densities. If higher density beings choose to interact, and a lower density being asks for an interaction, it is possible and often arranged.

We are speaking of free will and chosen identities. Within humanity resides an omnipresent God who can attune to all seven densities through the seven chakras, or seals. This is done by going within yourself, focusing on the higher chakras, and asking the God within to come forth. It takes quiet time, in a quiet place, preferably in nature, away from psychic turbulence and the judging eyes of your peers. It also takes patience, love and joy bent inward, which raises your vibratory frequency. It also heals the mental, emotional and physical bodies. You have the potential and the equipment to raise the vibratory frequency of the physical body into light, transcend all densities to the seventh, and bring it back again. That is how powerful you are.

Along the way through the higher densities, you will meet Orions, Pleiadians, Andromedans and a whole host of other diverse civilizations and their worlds. If you feel threatened by this, or are afraid of turning on your light, remember you don't have to. You, and only you, determine which density you choose to identify with and express upon. A question you might ask yourself is, "Why limit myself?"

The Earth exists in the third density, although the first and second densities are also present. What is unknown to most is that the fourth, fifth, sixth and seventh densities are also present. The third density is shifting in awareness to the fourth, which will reestablish love as the manifesting force behind all creation, all attitudes, all emotions, all actions on the lower densities. This is known as 'heaven on Earth.' It is when the gnomes and fairies come out to play along with other civilizations that have been aware of and residing alongside humanity for eons. This is the beginning of what is called "the age of God." It is the experience of a small fragment of grander things yet to come.

To further expand your knowledge concerning the universe, we must address the planes within the densities or dimensions. There are planes that exist within the dimensions, and there are planets and civilizations on those planes. So now you have the different densities or dimensions, the different planes within those densities or dimensions, and the planets and civilizations as well as other life forms within the planes. *It's a big universe!*

What the Earth and its inhabitants are experiencing now is a transitional period in which all creation not based upon love is crumbling, reorganizing and shifting into the next density. This includes your relationships, your jobs, attitudes and emotions toward self, others and the world in which you live. All attitudes, emotions, actions and their physical manifestations and counterparts must shift into the fourth density, which is love, to continue upon this plane. Government, religious and business institutions, humanity's physical, emotional and mental bodies and the environment itself-the very platform for life-are all cleansing, healing, restructuring, reorganizing and in some cases, departing to express somewhere else.

These are exciting and turbulent times, and the prize is worth it. It is behind door number four, and it is l o v e - a planet and society where love is the manifesting force behind all creation. What many ask is, "Who is doing this to me?" You are doing it to y o u - t h e part of you that resides in the fourth density along with the parts that reside in the fifth, sixth and seventh densities-not to mention all the other entities that reside upon the fourth, fifth, sixth and seventh densities who have intervened in the past to save the Earth. These entities are intervening once again to insure the survival of the planet and humanity as a species, a civilization which, as a collective, is bent upon destroying itself and the very platform of life that sustains it.

There are still the other dimensions and planes to engage, not to mention the planets and civilizations within those planes and dimensions.

You have to have the consciousness for it. You have to earn the right to engage higher consciousness. You do this by healing fear, unworthiness, lower vibrational attitudes and emotions, and turning on your light. This magnetizes the experience to you. Like attracts like, and light attracts light. There are people, like you, who have engaged seventh density entities by expanding in consciousness. Some remember and some forget because when you return to three-dimensional consciousness, it all seems like a dream. Do you think the higher-density entities thought you were a dream? Hardly. They can see all the way to the first density, and they remember that they have been doing so for eons and that you are a mixture of their seed and the Earth.

To Earth, these seventh density beings are known as archangels. They are known throughout the universe as Andromedans. They are omnipresent light beings who are overseers concerned for the evolution of humanity, a race known as half-God and half-human.

Astral Planes Between the Third & Fourth

When one expands into new territory and greater realities, there is a need for greater knowledge and self-authority. There is also a need for conscious contact with an Ascended Master in the beginning to aid you in healing and protection. In most cases, protection and guidance are there. But, there are times when one mistakenly attunes to lower astral levels. These levels have "faker" spirits who will tell you that they are great masters and have you do all sorts of things to make yourself holy or spiritual. They will also give you elaborate rituals and speak of hierarchies-all unnecessary when you know indeed that you are a God born of the original light.

Before taking a trip, it is wise to have a map, as well as someone who has traveled the road and knows the detours and places to avoid. Thus we are giving you a map, limited as it may be, to give you an understanding of the physical, emotional, mental and astral bodies, as well as the astral planes between the third and fourth dimensions.

Let us begin with the physical body, or lowest density mass. The Earth is God, and your body is also God. The physical body has a lower frequency, or density, yet it is still an expression of God-All That Is. It is holy ground. Within the body you have a soul equipped with a mental body, an emotional body, an astral body and an etheric body. There are bodies beyond the etheric body. As you move up or expand along this vibrational continuum, you will find yourself residing upon different planes and dimensions (or densities). You will also realize that you are not alone on these planes and dimensions.

Let us tour from the lowest to the highest vibrations. Upon leaving your physical body, your mental and emotional bodies continue in the astral body. The astral planes are very diverse. They exist between the third and fourth densities and are where the majority of people go upon their transition, or "death," as many call it. Death is also known as the wheel of life. Death is only final to those who believe it is and even then, it is only a sleep, not an ending. There are those who are laid out in what seem to be endless rows who refuse to wake up due to a dogmatic and ignorant teaching. They believe they must sleep eternally until Jesus comes to wake them and that the first one to come will be the devil to tempt them. Thus, they are shut down in consc10usness.

It is a very sad plane. You would do yourself and us a favor if you would dispense with this false belief and wake up here and now. You would also save us a lot of work. People who are filled with excessive fear, unworthiness, grief, anger, malevolence, confusion or any other lower vibrational attitudes and emotions go to the lower astral levels. The first astral levels, or planes, are very dark and gray, corresponding to the people existing there. As one moves up the astral planes, there is more light, more love and more compassion.

The mid-levels are filled with everyday people going about business as normal in astral bodies that are as real to them as their physical bodies once were. Everything upon their level is also real, or physical, to them. The astral realm is a mental realm. Consciousness creates reality instantly within the astral level. There is no lag time between thought and physical manifestation, as there is on Earth.

As one moves up into higher astral levels, there are many wise and gifted beings, yet they are still limited in their wisdom and teachings. They are still on the wheel of cyclic existence.

Before we continue we must advise against judgment or condemnation of the lower astral levels. They are in need of love, compassion and healing. The God flame exists within them also. It may be a spark, yet a spark can ignite the full flame at any time. No one has judged or condemned those lost souls. Consciousness creates reality in this life and the next, and your consciousness gravitates or magnetizes to a plane that matches its vibration. Your vibration is the totality of thought you have chosen to be your reality. Unconditional love and joy are thoughts of the highest vibration, and fear, anger, jealousy and the need to dominate, control or manipulate others are thoughts of the lowest vibration. There is a whole gray area in between. This ingenious system could only be created by God, for it honors free will and allows the individual to express, however they choose, on whatever level-while being loved unconditionally.

After a short while on the lower levels, most people realize the ignorance of harboring the lower vibrational attitudes and emotions. When they are ready, help is always there to heal and lift them into higher states of consciousness. However, this help never trespasses. It allows, until it is asked for.

There are those from the higher astral levels who attend to the lower astral levels, yet they, too, are learning from those beyond the astral levels. Beyond the astral levels lies the fourth dimension, which is love felt for all things, and the fifth dimension, the Christ consciousness. Here reside loving beings-the Beautiful Many Christed Masters-who administer to the needs of humanity. Their numbers are beyond counting, and they are not limited to the human experience.

We spoke earlier about the body being a physical adaptation to the environment. There are other planets with different embodiments and beings that are fully Christed within their embodiments. There are life forms that would seem ungodly to most humans, but within them resides a loving, joyous, wise and powerful Christed being. There are also those who ascended from the human experience and are no longer on the wheel of life. They are your known masters, saints and sages, of both genders, as well as quite a few unknown, ascended souls. Many ascended to a place known as Orion and others evolved even further to a place called Andromeda. They will be very active in the near future upon Earth.

In using words and a linear-time method to convey an understanding, there will always be limitation. These descriptions of the planes and dimensions are given to provide a map, yet everyone knows a map will only get you there. What you see and experience is up to you.

Manifesting & Engaging Contact

Consciousness creates reality. Therefore, to magnetize and engage a spirit or being of a higher vibration, one must first allow them to be a part of one's reality or consciousness. In other words, one must raise one's consciousness, which, in turn, opens the sacred senses. This allows the individual to sense the presence of unseen entities.

In raising one's consciousness, one has to overcome the collective consciousness based on the intellect-which does not want to go beyond its present awareness of believing in only the five senses and the greatest of all barriers: fear and unworthiness. A loving, joyous, courageous soul with an open mind is mandatory for contacting the higher vibrational realms.

The best model to explain the unseen planes and dimensions is the vibrational continuum. The physical body is the lowest density of God. The next vibration-the emotional and mental bodies-is within the astral level. In many cases, these lower astral levels are filled with lower vibrational attitudes and emotions and discarnate spirits that did not align with the higher vibrational aspects of self. Lower vibrational attitudes and emotions, such as fear, unworthiness, anger, guilt or karmic ties and unfinished business kept them from reaching the higher planes. They continue in the astral level. They have mental and emotional bodies, and they affect those inhabiting the Earth mentally and emotionally.

As we move up in vibration, we encounter the etheric self, or true soul, and expand upward into the higher vibrations. From the etheric self on up, the vibrational continuum consists of light beings or beings of higher consciousness. One can align the lower bodies with the higher bodies and truly experience heaven on Earth. To do this, there must be a clearing away of all lower vibrational attitudes and emotions within self. Call forward the God within you, and merge with the higher aspects of self. As you ascend levels in consciousness, you engage others of like mind on any particular level or vibration.

This can best be explained by an imaginary journey:

Aaron, feeling a need to engage his own higher self or an ascended master, decides to begin a spiritual quest. This quest begins with a retreat to a mountain forest-a quiet, natural setting free from psychic turbulence and the judging eyes of his peers.

Aaron finds himself expanding, feeling the unconditional love and non-judging nature of the forest. He spends days, weeks and eventually months expanding, releasing and meditating. Fear, unworthiness, wrong conclusions from past experiences and intellectual dogmas and 'isms' fall away. Eventually, all that is left is the true Aaron, at one with all life, expressing unencumbered as a loving, joyous, powerful, manifesting God.

This brilliant light descends from the mountain, returning to his family and friends. He tells them of great ships, etheric cities, strange lights, feelings and encounters with entities unseen. He is met with judgment and condemnation. He is told to "get real." The world he left is no longer his home.

Due to his heightened sensory awareness, Aaron feels all the negative thought forms, limiting mental concepts and psychic bonds. He even sees discarnate spirits, trapped by their own lower vibrational attitudes and emotions, influencing his friends. He tries to tell his friends, but he is met with extreme resentment and is accused of being in league with the devil.

Aaron now becomes an outcast from a world he once thought was a world of five-sensory experience. Now he is aware of all the unseen energies and entities at work on a multitude of levels. He also recognizes that not all unseen entities are in his highest and best good.

As always, help is there when called upon, and Aaron goes to the local coffee shop to think and reevaluate his experiences. He neither understands the experience he is undergoing nor does he have the spiritual tools necessary to deal with negative influences that affect his daily life, of which he was previously unaware.

As Aaron gazes across the room, sipping on his tea, he sees a man sitting at a table with a presence about him. The same unconditional love of the mountain forest surrounds and emanates from this man. He hears a voice in his head, which is more like a powerful thought, that says, "He has the tools you seek."

Aaron feels compelled (one might even say "pushed") to meet this man. A ten-minute argument with himself ensues, denying the voice and resisting the urge to engage the man. Aaron keeps asking himself, "What if he thinks I'm crazy? What if he knows nothing of spirit? What if _ ? What if _ ? What if..?" Aaron finally gains the courage to address the man. He stands and turns toward the table, only to find the table is now empty. Aaron throws his money on the table and rushes out the door to find the man standing there, just outside the door. He blurts out, "I heard a voice. It said you have the tools I seek."

The man smiled as he said, "Son, I could not leave the building, for I came to meet someone unknown to m e - I felt it. When I tried to leave, due to my own impatience and doubt, something would not let me. You are the one I am supposed to meet, and yes, I have the tools you seek."

The man told Aaron about discarnate spirits-lost souls that have been trapped between worlds due to excessive guilt, anger, fear, unworthiness or unfinished business. He also told Aaron about negative thought forms, limiting mental concepts and the race mind, or collective consciousness, that is riddled with negative thought forms and limiting mental concepts, as well as a host of other lower vibrational attitudes and emotions. He told Aaron that his greater sensitivity and awareness is a gift and that with the gift came responsibility and a great need for self-authority. He taught Aaron how to heal all negative influences with a few simple techniques, which if used in conjunction with his higher self or other ascended masters, would never fail. He taught Aaron to be discreet and to be very selective about those with whom he shared his greater understanding. He also told him to rise above the need for any love or acceptance outside of self. He impressed upon Aaron the importance and need for gifted ones to assist in healing lost souls, dissolving negative thought forms and limited mental concepts, and awakening humanity to a greater, more unlimited awareness and understanding of God and the universe.

He taught Aaron of humanity's greatest awareness: "Love is the only and ultimate power. Heal with love, call upon the power of love, and align yourself with love. The ascended ones come on the wings of love, and work through those who choose love."

The best way to engage an ascended one is to be an ascended one. Though you have a body, you are a spirit, liken unto God-a consciousness which is the one consciousness that encompasses all consciousness. To engage the higher aspects of self, the higher planes and dimensions and those who reside on these planes and dimensions, one must raise one's own vibration, or consciousness. Allow them to be a part of your greater reality. "As you believe, so it is."

The Six Great Liars

We desire to address the first five of the six great liars. They are the five senses. When the Gods entered the body, they entered a world in which the five senses were necessary to experience the physical vibration known as "mass." Their attention, or consciousness, became fully immersed in mass, and the five senses became tools for survival instead of tools for experience. In most cases, full attention to the five senses became necessary for survival.

Because of this, other spiritual senses became dull or unrecognizable. The gifts of clairvoyance, clairaudience and clairsentience faded away. Humanity could no longer see, hear or feel the other planes and dimensions, or the unconditional love of God. The spiritual senses were natural and common to the Gods before their descent into mass. They are still innate in humans, yet, like a muscle that is never used, they have atrophied. The major portion of humanity is in need of spiritual calisthenics-an exercise program to work out and awaken the spiritual senses.

Although man is surrounded by Gods and Goddesses, angels and fairies and a whole host of unseen intelligent beings, he is unaware of them. Faded spiritual senses allowed man to fool himself into believing he was alone. He also has felt that God and his spiritual friends have abandoned him. He cannot see them, hear them, touch them, or feel them with his five senses. Nonetheless, they are there, and they have always been there.

The sixth and greatest of all liars is the intellect. It takes in only what the five senses give it, denying the presence of anything beyond the five senses. It also has within it all of the fear, guilt, unworthiness, superstitious dogma, religious dogma, scientific dogma and wrong conclusions from past experience based upon input from the five senses. The intellect is armed with a myriad of excuses and denials to invalidate the awakening and opening of the spiritual senses. It needs to be in control.

To awaken the unique God within, one must:

1. Dispense with the lower vibrational attitudes, emotions and wrong conclusions.

2. Put the intellect in its proper place as the servant of spirit rather than the master.

3. Realize that the five senses are only a very small part of a multidimensional God.

How does one do this? "Put it in reverse." The same God that drove you into your limitations can drive you out. Will and desire are the vehicles to drive you into a greater reality.

The mind is a wonderful tool in the hands of spirit. It can get you to the gate. Yet feelings are the key. God is a feeling. Live by your feelings.

The Feminine God

In a time before my time as Ezekiel, the land was governed by simple people. They worshipped a feminine God and had many deities to represent different aspects of nature. They were gatherers and tillers of the soil. It was a time of peace, harmony, abundance and unity with all life. They worshipped and gave thanks to the feminine aspect of God for their abundant crops and the birth of all life, especially their children. They believed the feminine God to be the mother of all life, and all life was their family. They treated all life as their sacred family, and there was truly no separation between God, their people and nature.

To the west were the warring herdsmen. They worshipped their image of a masculine God of power. They believed the thunder to be his voice and lightening to be his wrath. Therefore, they put him in the ethers, away from the totality of life. They were conquerors and prayed to their image of God to bring them victory and give them strength in battle. They prayed that God would rage upon and punish their enemies. Their enemies consisted of anyone who had something they wanted.

The peaceful tillers of the soil were no match for the warring herdsmen, whose actions were incomprehensible to them. They could not bear arms against the warring herdsmen because they had no weapons and could not bring harm to anyone. To harm the herdsmen would be to harm their brothers, for they, too, were born of the one mother. Regardless of their ignorance and actions, the herdsmen were family. Thus, the tillers were conquered and enslaved by the herdsmen.

The herdsmen hated the feminine God who opposed their actions against humanity, nature, and life in general. The feminine God was a constant reminder of all they were not and what they knew in their heart of hearts to be true. They began a crusade to crush and destroy any trace of the feminine God. Temples and statues were destroyed. Those who worshipped the feminine God were either killed or tortured, and soon fear and intimidation erased all but a faint memory of the feminine God.

The warring herdsmen replaced the feminine God with their own image of a wrathful, punishing, masculine God, and their holy men created codes, doctrines, rules and regulations to appease this image. The beliefs and religions they created allowed them to continue to enslave and control the people, tax their goods and continue doing as they wished to humanity and nature.

After many generations, the warring, wrathful, punishing God became an accepted belief by the majority on Earth. This attracted the people of Elaga-extraterrestrials that assumed and acted out this image using their advanced technology to gain dominion over the Earth and its people. Those warring herdsmen who set out to conquer, control and enslave were soon conquered and controlled themselves due to their ignorance and the image they had created. The warring, wrathful, punishing God was now replaced by the people from Elaga.

The people from Elaga gave wrath and punishment a whole new meaning, and those who did not worship them were dealt with very severely. They had great ships with weaponry that decimated entire cities in a moment. Those who resisted became examples of a power that, according to their understanding, could be nothing other than God. It was, in truth, a technologically advanced, yet spiritually backward, people interacting with the people of Earth. This was the second phase of the fictitious image of a wrathful, punishing God. The Pharisees were the third.

This understanding is dedicated to the Women of Spirit and the feminine God-that which births and is the mother of all life, that which is returning to nurture and give birth to a new life-one of love, joy, peace and unity with all life.

Images, Religions, Symbols

It is written that man is created in the same image and likeness of God. To fully understand this, let us replace "image" with "consciousness." There are many small minds that have taken their own personal image of God and projected that image into the ethers. This image has inherent within it all of the limitations of the one projecting the image. In order to give this image validity, they seek the support and agreement of others. Those who have no image agree with them and gather around this image, and thus is born organized religion. The reason that there are over 11,000 religions is because there are over 11,000 images.

In most cases the image is passed down by humans, generation to generation, where it is altered according to the needs of the existing government and religious organizations. God-inspired or not, humans are fallible. The clarity of any truth is relative to the clarity of the mind it comes through. All experience is altered by the one who perceives it. An experience must fit one's picture of reality and if it does not, an individual will adjust the experience within the mind. He will then relay the experience as he perceived it. If one does not have anything to compare an experience with, he will adjust the experience to symbols and images he understands. Many sacred writings were not recorded until 200 years after the events, according to stories passed down by word of mouth. We all know what happens to the original story. It is altered, amended and adjusted to fit the needs of the storyteller.

There are tribes in Africa that have built straw airplanes and lit fires to attract the Gods in the sky. To the tribesmen, anyone who can fly must be a God. When they see airplanes fly overhead, they believe the airplanes are Gods. Those in the airplane understand and accept the airplane as a mechanical means of traveling long distances.

As Ezekiel, I experienced the landing of a ship. The ship was from Elaga, a technologically advanced civilization. They had the ability to teleport objects and people and communicate with anyone, anywhere, at any time. They desired to "straighten out" humanity in their own way. Unfortunately, they also wanted to be appreciated and worshipped as Gods. Their love was far from unconditional. I described this ship to the best of my ability, and it is recorded in your bible, along with countless other encounters with "fiery chariots."

This was an intellectual description by a personality and was based upon the experience of that lifetime. The description was based on my understanding at that time of God and the universe, using the words, symbols and objects understood at that time. In other words, it is old news.

I have since evolved to a greater understanding of God and the universe. I now know about the Elaga civilization and their technology. What I experienced as Ezekiel and my "superstition" has been dissolved by this greater understanding of God and the universe. Images and religious misconceptions based upon the old images give way to this greater understanding. To hold on to the images of the past is to hold on to ignorance. Humanity is evolving into a greater understanding of God, the universe and the other planes, dimensions and civilizations that are in the universe. To come to this understanding, we must dispense with the misperceptions, superstitions and graven images of the past and open our hearts and minds to a greater reality.

I desire, if you wish, for you to read the book of Ezekiel within your Bible in light of this new understanding. The leader of the people from Elaga was named Jehovah. He was known as the jealous, wrathful God of Israel. In order to intimidate the people into worshipping him as their only God, he unleashed shattering and devastating weapons upon all who resisted his edicts or his self-ordained role as the God of Israel.

Upon his orders, six men of Elaga with their shattering weapons, which were atomic in nature, annihilated the men, women and children of Israel, leaving only a few terrified survivors to spread the news. Another man from Elaga dressed in linen was ordered to reach into the bowels of one of the smaller ships, known as "cherubim," and take hot coals (radioactive material) and spread them all about the city. This was to insure Jehovah's prophesy that a plague would come upon the city, causing people's hair and fingernails to fall out. He prophesied that they, and all who came years after would die and become food for the beasts and ravens. His wrath was not limited to the people of Israel, for he destroyed other cities as well. It was a reign of terror and mass genocide.

This knowledge will come as a shock to a great many of you. Some will deny it; some will remember the experience-for it was part of their former experience-and feel victimized or angry.

Reason this: What kind of God would do such a thing? Is it a God you can look up to and worship? Only a limited God would see himself as separate from humanity and order mass genocide, demand sacrifice of children, birds and beasts, and demand offerings of oils, grains and herbs. Reason this: Would it make sense for a God, an omnipresent God of pure, unconditional love and joy, to war upon itself? Who would he root for or side with? He would be against himself-punishing and killing himself. A singular entity with an ego that believes itself to be separate from, or above, the whole of life is not embracing the totality of omnipresent God.

The encounters between Jehovah and the human race have been the foundation for several of your great religions, the inspiration for much of the Old Testament, and they are one of the grandest of all misperceptions. Jehovah was a technologically evolved tyrant who was spiritually backward. He had a great ship-described in depth to the best of my ability, as Ezekiel, according to the knowledge of that time period. He also had the smaller ships known as "cherubim." They sounded like a great roar of rushing waters when they ascended and descended. On these ships were powerful, shattering, atomic weapons that were used on all who resisted.

Jehovah was the force behind Joshua and David. He created a weapon of terror beyond your wildest dreams. Those who encountered it where hideously turned inside out. Their hair and fingers fell from their bodies, their bodies literally exploded, and those who survived prayed for death. This terrible weapon, along with a great ship, warred against innocent and peaceful people who had nothing but a sword and shield. Jehovah's armies were merciless and their slaughter was all done in the name of G o d - a jealous, wrathful God who would have no other images before him. Jehovah forced those who would not deliver his message to eat their dung and urine, or he took away their kin to insure the delivery of his message. Jehovah was a God who warred upon and hated the white man, the black man, the red man and all who where not of his chosen people. He killed and tortured his own people for not perfectly obeying and carrying out his demands. He was truly merciless, unforgiving, and had no respect for life, not even the lives of his own followers. Fear, intimidation, control and manipulation were the tools of Jehovah.

These tools are still used today. Many of your religions are based upon the doctrines of Jehovah-doctrines that in the past were enforced by a jealous, wrathful and technologically evolved tyrant. Many of the doctrines were fair and just, and they assisted humanity in establishing a 'moral' code of behavior that allowed them to coexist peacefully. But, the image of God left behind has severely stunted a great portion of humanity's spiritual evolution. Fear, unworthiness and the image of a jealous, wrathful and embittered God that no one can appease and who exists somewhere in the ethers are the great separators and stumbling blocks to awakening and uniting with the one consciousness that encompasses all consciousness.

Who would want to unite, become one with, or serve such an image? Many, in ignorance and through fear and intimidation, have become subservient to just such an image and to those religious institutions that perpetuate such an image. It has become very profitable to move God out of the hearts and minds of people and to use fear, intimidation and guilt to demand payment to appease a wrathful, punishing image.

The pure, unconditional love and joy of God is not to be earned or bought. It is something to become one with. The temple is within. It has always been within. It is my desire that you contemplate this experience and use whatever techniques work for you to process and release any lower vibrational attitudes and emotions you may be experiencing. This knowledge is given for that purpose-to get you beyond your fear, unworthiness, misperceptions and wrong conclusions from this or other experiences at the hands of those who, in ignorance, are perpetuating the wrathful, punishing, controlling and manipulating image of God.

Finally, in this regard, a comment concerning a group known as the "Jehovah's Witnesses" and any other religious institution which fosters an image of a wrathful, punishing God, separate from humanity and nature, living somewhere in the ethers. They are not to be warred upon. They are to be loved. If they have experienced the wrath of Jehovah in a past life or the wrath of misguided, overzealous individuals perpetuating the image of a wrathful, punishing God, they have much to overcome. Many of them are aligned with Jesus, Yaweh, and the Great White Brotherhood and are just using the wrong name, and that is all right.

Those whose hearts are filled with love for humanity and nature are on track no matter what their image. I am empathic with those who falsely align with and perpetuate the wrathful punishing God. I understand the fear, the unworthiness and the confusion. I understand the scars and misperceptions that came from these encounters. I, too, was once confused and deeply scarred from those experiences. I have since healed my wounds. The fear, unworthiness and confusion have settled into my soul as wisdom. It is my deepest desire that all humanity heal and awaken also.

The prize is unconditional love, pure joy and a oneness with the omnipresent source of all consciousness and all life. Only a fool would not trade their graven images, their fear and unworthiness, and the pain and suffering which comes from ignorance.

Pure unconditional love and joy is pressing hard upon all humanity. Those who need an image to worship outside of themselves should choose an image that empowers them and reminds them of what resides within self. They should choose an image they can love and aspire towards becoming one without an image that intimidates them or makes them fearful. Over and over again, we have given the image of a loving, joyous God to humanity. This image has been bent and twisted by humans and their institutions.

In the days to come, all will be aligned with a new image that honors all paths and all people as unique expressions of God. This new image will also incorporate nature as a part of the whole that is to be loved and cherished. This will be the Golden Age, the thousand years of peace. The Golden Light that is pure, unconditional love and joy will fill the hearts of all humanity. That is destiny.

The Gods of Love & Peace

This next understanding concerns another highly evolved being, named "Yahweh," and the Great White Brotherhood. Yahweh was the God of love and peace. There was, and still is today, a Great White Brotherhood-a collection of ascended saints, sages and masters who have greatly loved and served humanity for eons. They are loving, peaceful masters who have been overseers of humanity's spiritual evolution. They do not believe in war and are greatly loved. They were a threat to Jehovah's desire to be the one sovereign God of Israel and the entire planet. They pleaded to Jehovah to end his senseless slaughter and allow humanity its own evolutionary process. They even stood in front of his ships, which greatly angered Jehovah, for his weapons could not harm them.

They were unseen by people on Earth, yet they were present throughout Jehovah's reign. They prayed incessantly to the Supreme Intelligence, the Creator of all that is, and one day a great ship appeared in the heavens. It was brighter than ten thousand suns. It was swifter than anything known, and on it were the greatest of all Gods that ever were. Jehovah was intimidated by this great ship and utterly defenseless, for he could do nothing against it. He fled to a far distant galaxy, never to return. Yahweh and the 13 grand masters of the Great White Brotherhood began what was, and is to this day, the arduous task of healing the scars, wounds and misperceptions created from the encounter with Jehovah.

They sent dreams of peace and visions of brotherly love. They sent one of their own, endowed with the love, wisdom and power of Yahweh and the thirteen. They transferred their combined higher consciousness and energy into one singular entity. The star of Bethlehem was a great ship that oversaw the birth of this entity, holding its position while the rest of the stars traversed the heavens. He taught of love, peace and brotherhood and his forgiveness and mercy were unlimited. He was the son of Joseph and Mary, indeed an immaculate conception, and he was known to you as "Jesus." There shall come a great light, very soon in your time, that will once and for all heal the scars and images of the past. It will sever all connections with Jehovah, which still exist to this day. The days of controlling, manipulating energies will come to a close. The pure unconditional love and joy ofYaweh and the Great White Brotherhood will be the governing consciousness of humanity.

The Last Great War

The last great war shall be a war in consciousness, light and energy. There shall be no nuclear war. There is a limit to allowing, and nuclear war would be devastating to other life forms on this plane and other dimensions as well. It shall not be permitted. The last great war shall be between the Christ Consciousness and all that which is against the Christ Consciousness. It is a war between the soul's ego, being the working duplicate of the God-self, and the alter ego, programmed by social consciousness. The alter ego is riddled with fear, unworthiness, disease, religious and scientific dogma, and a myriad of wrong conclusions from past experiences. There will be those who will resist vehemently the awakening and healing process, yet it is no longer optional. It is destiny.

The fruits of the labor of grand masters, saints and sages are being harvested as we speak, with the greater harvest just around the comer. This great war shall be multidimensional, as above, so below. It will be experienced on Earth as the fall of the tyrants. Those who lust for power and money at the expense of humanity and nature, those who desire to possess, dominate, control and manipulate, and those who refuse to honor the divine right to free will and self-determination of the individual, shall not see the coming age. The lag time between the action and the reaction is being drastically shortened. Their karma shall seem instantaneous. Those who cling to social consciousness will also experience an acceleration of everything within social consc10usness.

The diseases, fears, insecurities, anger, violence, jealousies, separating attitudes and emotions will all manifest until there is a healing and change in consciousness. Those in your governments and your business and religious institutions who desire to dominate, control and manipulate, stifling individual freedom, will become even more tyrannical and fanatical. The other polarity will also be amplified, and those who stand steadfast for love of God, humanity and nature, as well as universal justice, will also be exalted. Behind them will be legions seen and unseen. The masses will become enlightened and empowered from within, and they shall also make their stand. The polarities between love, joy and individual freedom and the opposing factions of fear, againstness and those who desire to take away your freedom will become very apparent.

Nature will also move with the acceleration of time in her cleansing and healing process, and there will be a quantum leap in physical evolution. There has been an electrical band of energy, known as the blue corona, placed around the Earth, which is accelerating and amplifying the awakening and healing process. It is intensifying the polarities, exalting everything and bringing forward the people and events into your daily lives that correspond with your attitudes and emotions. You are all getting a crash course in self. As the energy increases cyclically and exponentially, it will seem as if the world has gone rather mad.

This event is also happening on what is termed other planes and dimensions as well. The astral levels, often referred to as the wheel of life, are also experiencing the awakening and healing process. They, too, are experiencing a quickening of their attitudes and emotions.

As the veils are lifted, many are going to experience feeling the presence of loved ones who have made their transition working out unfinished business, or just saying good-bye as they ascend to new levels. They are also healing the wounds, traumas and wrong conclusions from past experiences, which also perhaps involved those they left behind on Earth, yet are still connected to on a mental and emotional level.

There is another experience that is going to manifest in your heavens. It will be the greatest of all wars. It concerns a group of beings that have, and still are, based upon the Earth. They were responsible for creating great dynasties. They have been behind the greatest tyrants that have plagued the Earth for eons. They have created images of jealous wrathful Gods, fearful demons and a few other clever creations-all to keep you in darkness and subservience. They do love humanity, yet that love is very conditional, and they will only exalt you to the level that they can be worshipped and continue to control and manipulate you. They do not desire for you to realize that you are Gods born of the original light, for then they would have no more control and could no longer hold their exalted position over you. They are best understood as a house of consciousness, and there are many who have mistakenly aligned themselves with this house and are, in most cases, unconscious that they are doing their bidding. They are unaware that when you desire to control and manipulate others, you attune to and attract others of like mind, on other planes and dimensions of consciousness. In turn for the use of a little of the power from these malevolent beings, they themselves end up being controlled and manipulated, and in some cases, possessed.

Like minds attract like minds. These particular entities are known as the evolved tyrants. Those who align themselves with this house will be known by their own desires to hold others beneath them and their controlling and by manipulating tendencies. These evolved tyrants are realizing their next move is governed by the moves of those beneath them. Thus, they have given up their freedom and are controlled in truth by those beneath them. They are also evolving and coming to the realization that they do not need to possess so many forgotten Gods to exact self worth. Those based upon the Earth are already being turned around. There is a greater consciousness intervening on your behalf, along with a great armada with ships beyond your wildest imagination. Their leader, the once defeated Jehovah, is returning. Yet, you will not experience his wrath, for that which awaits him is awesome. It will be as if the greatest of all Gods that ever were and the whole universe have set out to greet him on your behalf. That is how greatly you are loved. There shall be a war in the heavens, and it will be a war of consciousness and light.

On Earth it will be seen as great bursts of light in your heavens, eventually ending in twelve days of continuous light. This will signal the end of the tyrants, the end of social (nonspiritual) consciousness and all lower vibrational attitudes and emotions. This will be the final lifting, and those who are left will be the meek, profound feeling entities who have aligned themselves with their soul's purpose and destiny and chose love to be the manifesting force behind all creation. They will be those who removed themselves from social consciousness and chose the Christ consciousness-those who aligned themselves with the house of Yaweh, the Great White Brother/Sisterhood, and the Beautiful Many masters, saints, and sages dedicated to awakening the God within you. It will be known as the age of God.

Proof

I wish to speak concerning the desire for proof. You will only see what you want to see, hear what you want to hear, and accept what you want to accept. You, and only you, authorize what is to be your reality. The universe unfolds according to your picture of reality. Those whose minds are closed, or who are extremely skeptical, do not want proof. What they desire is to remain in their present reality. And, as God's favorite words are, "As you wish," there they stay. Their world is a reflection of a closed and skeptical mind, which is manifesting and validating their truth.

Another point concerning truth is that if a truth needs defending, you don't own it. If you are in need of acceptance from others, you have given away your power. Only a limited God needs defending. Cast your pearls only before those who will appreciate them, and if they are of a different truth, allow them.

This can best be illustrated by a story:

A small-minded professor once came to a great master. He was very closed to any reality other than that which could be measured or experienced by the five senses. He demanded that the master read his mind to prove to him his spiritual abilities. The master smiled, and, pulling a small straight pin from his robe, he asked the professor to first read the inscription upon the head of the pin. The professor stared and stared. He took his glasses off and cleaned them, then once again stared intently upon the head of the pin. After a few minutes, the professor said, "I know something is there, but I can't read it. It's just too small." The master replied, "That is also my problem."

The professor, oblivious to the correlation between the small pin and his small mind, asked, "Can I take it home with me and use a magnifying glass on it?" The master replied, "I am the magnifying glass you seek." This again puzzled the professor. The master plucked the pin from his hand, stared at it and read the following inscription: "The Universe cannot be held on the head of a pin."

The professor, again missing the wisdom in the words of the inscription, accused the master of already knowing the inscription or making it up. The master replied, "I had foreknowledge of the inscription. A greater master gave me the pin and asked me to read the inscription. I spent days in contemplation until it was finally revealed to me. I told the great master the inscription, and he smiled and nodded his head in agreement."

The professor replied, "So you have never used a microscope or magnifying glass to prove it to yourself?" The Master replied, "I told you before, I am the magnifying glass, and I have seen the inscription-not with my physical eyes, but with my inner vision. It is all the proof I need. You, dear brother, shall never know what is on the head of the pin, for you have not learned to trust your own feelings and knowingness."

"You have gained your understanding through recycled ignorance and that which can be stuffed into a test tube or measured by a physical apparatus. A fact is nothing more than a theory that enough people have agreed upon. Even imagination is a fact relative to the plane upon which it resides. All things begin as an idea or thought, and as we evolve in consciousness, truth evolves and facts change. As for reading your mind, I will tell you this. You will waste a great portion of your future thoughts wondering what was on the head of the pin. The universe is only as infinite as the mind that can perceive it. If you say it is so, it is so to you. Truly, as you believe, so it is. I cannot read your mind until you open it." The Master stuck the pin in his robe and joyously went his way.

"For in this place, the Father cannot do any great thing because they lack the faith."-Jesus

God Is

We have spoken of the past and given you a clear image of what God is not. Therefore, it is time to give you a less limited perception of what God is. In doing this, you will have something to hold up to the many idols and graven images of the past. This perception is also limited. To believe that the totality of God can be written or spoken is an error. What is infinite cannot be understood or contained within the finite mind of humans. It is only when you expand beyond the mind that your image expands. God is only as infinite as the mind that perceives Him. We desire for you to feel these words, for they carry with them more than what is written.

This journey will not be made in a linear movement, but rather one that goes inward and outward, up and down, backwards and forwards, and from the finite to the infinite. A helpful hint in this understanding is that infinity travels in many directions.

The Father-Mother-God principle, known as 'life,' is the one consciousness that encompasses all consciousness, which is omnipresent on all planes and all dimensions throughout the universe-uni(one) verse(song).

God is the nothingness of space, as well as all that is contained in space. God is neither male nor female, yet God is both male and female. God is the infinite universe and the billions of worlds in the infinite atoms. God is the fly you splattered on your window. God is the distant star in the heavens. God is the Milky Way, as well as the grain of sand on the beach. God is the flower, the tree, the dolphin, the toad, the fish, the rock. God is life in all of its forms, on all planes and all dimensions. There is nothing that is not vibrating and pulsing with the love of God, for it is love that holds it together. Even you, regardless of how you judge yourself, are God. No matter how hard you try, you cannot separate yourself or any living thing from omnipresence. God is all that is and in his most unlimited understanding; God is pure, unconditional love and joy. This could go on forever just as God is forever.

There is one example which best represents the "is" that is all that is, and it rises in the east every morning. It shines its light on everything and judges nothing. Its rays warm the rich and the poor, the honest and the lying, the snake as well as the eagle. Its rays of love are given unconditionally, regardless of attitude or form. It is ongoing and never ceases.

It knows there is nothing worth stepping out of unconditional love and joy. Be like the sun. Greet the sun and give it thanks for being the example, just as you would greet and thank Jesus for his example. And know that this example is there for you to become. Only a limited God would have only one son. You are all sons and daughters of the Most High. In reality, you are the Most High, for in this image you were created. Do not separate yourself from God or the universe any longer. It is written, "Know you not that you are the temple of God and that the spirit of God dwells in you?" (Corinthians 3:16) You can choose another reality, but it is only an adventure into illusion and the limitations inherent in it. Be one with the infinite, for in God there is no separation. Let the pure, unconditional love and joy permeate your being until all is lifted into oneness. Become the light, for out of light you were born and into light you shall return.

Satan & the Antichrist

Many of your sacred books were written in dark and superstitious times. There were great masters who had to use the terminology of the times, acknowledging the evolutionary stage of the people they were administering to. I once tried to bring a higher understanding to a man who was quite primitive in his understanding. This understanding was concerning the nature of our ships. He asked how they flew. I told him it was antigravity generated by a perpetual motion machine that was not limited to time, distance and space. He then asked what gravity and perpetual motion were.

I was getting nowhere fast. So, I told him the ship was a vehicle of the Gods, and it went where they wished because they commanded it so. This he understood. A simple man with no technological background will accept an act of God before he accepts a technological description of what he perceives as a phenomenon. To him it is the descent of a God. To us it is one of our vehicles landing. I am telling you this to give you an example of how many phenomena were recorded by primitive people and how, in order to convey a message, great masters had to use the language of humanity's technologically limited understanding.

Satan and the Antichrist are superstitious understandings representing the shadow side of man and woman. Humanity has an ego and an alter ego. Your soul's ego is pure and is the working duplicate of the loving, joyous, compassionate and powerful manifesting God that created it. Your alter ego is riddled with fear, anger, againstness, separation, scientific and religious dogma and a whole host of lower vibrational attitudes and emotions, as well as limiting mental concepts-such as Satan.

Satan and the Antichrist are representative of the shadow side of humans. The Antichrist is all that which is against the Christ consciousness coming forward within the individual. It is all that which is altered from the Christ consciousness, and it resides within the soul as the alter ego. The great war between the Christ and the Antichrist is the war between the soul's true ego and the alter ego. It is a war within self

It is experienced in the outer world as will operating from the soul's true ego, using love as the manifesting force behind all creation and cherishing humanity and nature, versus will operating from the baser alter ego using fear, selfishness and againstness, usually at the expense of humanity and nature. We cannot blame Satan or the Antichrist for our realities created by our own consciousness, thoughts and actions. If you want to war against Satan, clean up your consciousness. When you are free from all fear, anger, againstness, separation and judgment, you will see he no longer exists. All you will experience is omnipresent God. "As you believe, so it is."

If you believe in Satan, you create this evil within your mind. Many worship Satan by constantly looking for him. He is alive within their own mind. If Satan is no longer within your consciousness, he will not be a part of your reality. That is why it is written, "Resist not evil." People have performed hellish acts in the name of G o d - chastising, stoning, banning and killing other people and prophets. There have been more people killed in the name of God defending doctrines and images than were ever saved. Jesus himself was chastised, stoned and rebuked for doing the work of Satan. His persecutors never contemplated whom they were serving by their hellish deeds or whose children they were abusing. It is the alter ego and the superstitious, dogmatic, institutions founded upon fear, unworthiness, misperceptions and wrong conclusions from past experience that serve the Antichrist.

The Christ is not a singular entity. It is a state of consciousness where man knows himself to be God and God knows himself to be man. It is total immersion in the unique God born of the original light, your true, eternal and everlasting self. It is oneness with the unique, loving, joyous, compassionate, powerful manifesting God of your origin. It has great love for humanity and nature because it is all part of the omnipresent one.

The Antichrist is anything "anti" the union with God, and Satan can best be represented by the altered ego, that fearful, unworthy, judging, separating, voice within self, that part of self the light has not yet reached-the illusionary self.

Karma & the Wheel

In the most unlimited truth, karma does not exist. When one has merged with the pure essence of being, "the Christ nature," "the Buddha nature," or "total immersion and union with God," karma is finished. One lives by the law of grace and forgiveness. There is a simple truth given by a wonderful entity: "A man has got to know his limits." (Clint Eastwood) Although within each and every one of you is a loving, joyous, powerful, unlimited and manifesting God, not many have realized this God. Therefore, you create karma. Karma is better understood as the action/reaction principle or, "As you sow, so shall you reap." Like attracts like, and one magnetizes people and events to his life according to his consciousness. There are many that have built their kingdoms at the expense of humanity and nature. They act selfishly, arrogantly and without respect for man or beast. They soon find themselves surrounded by other selfish, arrogant or unloving people plotting to steal their kingdom, which eventually divides and collapses. It was built upon ignorance and a false foundation. There is also collective karma where towns, cities and nations are involved. Humanity as a whole has set into motion planetary events, due to their constant warring and abuse of humanity and nature.

There are those who deem themselves very clever because they have stayed a step ahead of the wolves or the competition, outwitting them at every corner. They never realized that they have outwitted themselves. They have ignorantly created a hell with ravishing beasts awaiting them. They have never asked themselves if they are happy, if the fruits of their labor bring them joy. They have never contemplated the concepts of "love," "compassion" or "impeccable integrity" in their interactions with humanity and nature. They are caught in the cycle of endless rebirth, and that rebirth will be with the same consciousness creating the same miserable and unfulfilled reality. Different places, different faces, different time, same circumstances, same consciousness. Every thought creates a reality, every action creates a reaction, and like attracts like. There are those who have separated themselves from humanity and nature, yet they have not separated themselves from their karma or the reactions to their actions. When their transgressions come home to roost, they seldom link the experience to their former thoughts or actions.

They say that they will be a little more clever and guard against that the next time. The safeguard is usually a physical means or a legal document or physical protection of some kind. You cannot hide or find shelter or protection from your consciousness. Your consciousness creates your reality.

Consciousness is a precious gift. It is the grandest treasure of all, yet many defile their consciousness daily with thoughts of fear, anger, jealousy, againstness and a whole myriad of other baser attitudes and emotions. These baser attitudes and emotions, along with the actions that follow them, create your tomorrow. Loving, joyous, caring and selfless attitudes and emotions, and the corresponding actions, also create your tomorrow. It is your divine right of free will to choose your tomorrow. If you want to clean up your world, clean up your consciousness. If you want to experience greater expressions of love, joy and beauty of the heavens, then create a consciousness that will magnetize it to you. Heaven or hell can be created right here on this plane of demonstration according to your consciousness.

In your passing, if you want to experience heaven, you must have the consciousness for it. The same goes for the other side of the coin. Those who have nurtured a hellish consciousness will create a continuance of the reality created by their own consciousness in the mental planes after their passing.

And where is God throughout this drama? God is the drama. God is the people and events, the platform for your drama. And God is loving you unconditionally, becoming your chosen realities. Be aware of your thoughts and your actions, and be kind to all sentient life. Your future depends upon it.

"A fool and his mischief is like fresh milk-it takes a little time to sour, but as surely as the cart follows the ox that pulls it, it will catch up." (Buddha)

Prophets, Disciples & Saints

Many of the prophets, disciples and saints of the past are walking among you in the present. Some have awakened as to their identity, some have not. One may be your gardener, your plumber, the school janitor, the bum-it could even be you. We all choose roles for the experiences they have to offer. I have entertained a myriad of expressions. I have been the priest, the lama, the yogi, the monk, the warrior, the shaman, the beggar, the bandit, the cripple and have worn a whole host of other identities. Why? For the experience.

You will never truly understand any expression until you have experienced it. Through experience one also gains the wisdom that enables one to have love and compassion for others. At the core of every man and woman is an eternal and unique, loving, joyous G o d - no matter how vile or ugly the outer expression. There is also the desire to remember.

Many masters have awakened to their true identity, yet they are barred from the very religious organizations created in their names. They are ignored, chastised and often killed by their own people. They are a threat to the positions, power, graven images and idols of the organizations. Where would organizations be if everyone knew that God loved them unconditionally, that God was within them and not in the ethers, and that you cannot buy or earn what is given freely?

You can see why the masters are a threat and the necessity for their removal. This pattern has been going on for eons. The Pharisees were a grand example of an organization of men who worshipped their positions, fine wine and the false power of money over truth. The Pharisees continued to perpetuate the image of a wrathful, punishing God somewhere in the ethers-the image left by the negative encounter with Jehovah. They found they could use this image to amass great wealth. All the Pharisees had to do was to remove God from man, put God in the ethers and tell man they and they alone knew God's edicts. This allowed the Pharisees to play upon the fear, unworthiness and ignorance of the people. This also allowed them to deliver the edicts of Jehovah, demand payments, and enslave and control the people.

Those who questioned or refused to pay were excommunicated or threatened with losing favor in the eyes of God. Others were condemned to eternal suffering at the hands of another fictitious entity, "the devil," in another fictitious place, "hell." Heaven and hell are states of consciousness, and consciousness creates reality. This includes past, present and future experience.

The jealous, wrathful God, the devil and hell are all misperceptions, fictitious entities and places based upon fear and ignorance. They are false idols and graven images that must be healed and released before humanity can evolve into oneness with the unique, loving, joyous God within. What of the Pharisees? They exist to this day. They have changed names, but many continue knowingly and unknowingly to perpetuate the graven images of the past. They, too, must release these images in favor of a God of pure, unconditional love and joy, omnipresent in all humanity and the totality of life. Congregations are diminishing this hour, and organizations will collapse upon themselves, for their foundation is fear. The pure, unconditional love and joy of God is coming upon this plane from within and without. Fear, unworthiness and ignorance will soon be a thing of the past. Humanity and its organizations must adjust to the flow.

How do I feel about the Pharisees of today? I love them and understand them. I was once misled. I understand the temptation of power and wealth. I also understand the true nature of God that will eventually be a planetary understanding that will no longer allow manipulation and enslavement of the masses.

The Gift of Jesus

When Jesus came to this plane, he was born of man. When asked who he was in the beginning, he said, "I am the Son of man." Later in his sojourn, he announced that he was a messenger of God. Further along his path, he realized he was the son of God. His last statement was, *"I am God."*

Jesus was an example of the Christ mind fully realized upon the Earth. It is written, "Ye are Gods, and the spirit of God dwells in you." It is also written, "The light that lights every man is the light of God." Jesus was the example of the light of God manifest. This light, or consciousness, resides within all humanity. It is often buried deeply beneath layers of fear, unworthiness, dogmas and a whole host of wrong conclusions from past experience.

The Christ or Christos is the union between God and man. It is where man knows himself to be God and God knows himself to be man. It is God in the flesh. Another term, "Emmanuel" means "God with us." They are all terms of "atonement." Jesus spoke the words, "I of myself do nothing, but the Father doeth the works." And, "I and the Father are one." These are examples of total immersion in allowing God to work through the fully attuned and aligned personality-in this case, Jesus. There have been many personalities that have fully attuned and aligned with God, thus allowing God to deliver unique messages to different people and cultures. Yet, the messages always expressed the nature of God, which is love.

These messages were often distorted and used to fulfill the wishes of kings and religious institutions, but you can easily recognize these distortions by measuring them against the mission of the masters.

This mission is to lift and empower individuals to honor each other as unique expressions of God, and to behave as if the God in all life matters. They all stand for individual God, individual freedom, and love of God, humanity and nature.

Many cultures believe that their prophets or masters are "the way," but it is the nature of God, expressed through the masters or prophets, that is the way. That same nature is within all. The masters are reminders; they are humble, and they love life profoundly. There is a saying attributed to Jesus, "I am the way, the truth and the light. No man shall enter heaven but by me."

The "I am" is the same "I am" God that spoke through many prophets and masters. They are all reminders and examples of the way. Jesus said, "Ye will do greater works than I, for I go on to the Father. You will never do greater works until you stop worshipping a personality. You will never become one with God, or the Christ consciousness that Jesus represented, until you find it within self. No matter what or whom you worship, you will never do the greater works because you will always be waiting for someone else to do it outside of yourself. The prayer Jesus most often used was, "Father, let them be one as we are one."

Jesus conquered his fears, unworthiness and confusion, thus walking a path for all people to walk. One of the greatest fears facing humanity is death. Yet, Jesus overcame not only the fear of death, but death itself. It was his desire to free humanity from the yoke of oppressive governments and traditions based upon superstition and ignorance. It was also his desire to burn the images of a wrathful, punishing God in favor of a God of unconditional love, joy, compassion and mercy. His greatest desire of all was to take God out of the ethers and the temples and reinstate God in his rightful place, which is in the hearts and minds of all humanity-and for this Jesus was crucified.

Even upon the cross, after being beaten, tortured, publicly humiliated and crucified, his last statement was, "Father forgive them for they know not what they do." His last deed was to heal the Roman who pierced his side with a spear. His love was unconditional. He was an example of courage, compassion, forgiveness and mercy-an example of God. Where is he today? He is in an omnipresent light body continuing his mission, reaching out to all who choose love-love of God, love of humanity, love of nature. He is one with God, and he is within the hearts and minds of all who choose love-all who rise above their fears, unworthiness and superstitions to become one as he became one.

Jesus is spearheading, so to speak, a divine plan, the first part of which was his Earthly sojourn to set the pattern and example. The second phase will be done through the hearts and minds of men. It is the second coming, or the Christ consciousness realized individually. This consciousness is emerging throughout all life. He is here to burn the false images in favor of an omnipresent image of God that includes the totality of life.

Jesus is the guidance and the power that resists man's graven images, ever lifting and empowering those who resist the false images of even himself. So when you feel the power to resist dogmas, "isms," schisms and the images flowing through you, know that it is the love of God, the love of Jesus, and that you are right on track, regardless of the judgments and condemnations of others. You didn't realize Jesus is with you all the time, loving you unconditionally and empowering the omnipresent individual God within you, now did you?

Jesus is not alone in this endeavor. He is with legions-the Beautiful Many Angelic Guides and Ascended Masters, Nature Spirits and other spiritually and technologically advanced civilizations are all coming together for a grand event. It is as if the whole universe has come to watch and assist in the birth of a planet and its people into a new time, another dimension and another place in the universe.

The Purpose of a Master

The purpose of a master is not to bind you to doctrines, "isms" and schisms. It is not to create an image somewhere in the ethers outside of humans or nature. It is not to create a following, thus ensnaring the masses. The purpose of a master is to lift and empower the individual, awakening the unique, loving, joyous, wise and powerful manifesting God in you. Those who gather around the true masters are not codependent. They are independent and unique. They share a common interest.

Many masters have come to this plane with the same message. They each deliver it in their own unique way, using words and symbols that cater to the many diverse cultures. The universal truths have always been part of their teachings. They all speak of an omnipresent, omnipotent, omniscient God, yet each places this God within the individual. They all speak of a heaven that is their home, yet they also say that heaven is a state of consciousness. They speak of love, joy and harmlessness. A great many of them realized God in nature while sitting beneath a tree.

Their teachings are simple, for they are simple in nature, uncluttered by the psychobabble of intellectual rhetoric. They played and meditated. They surrendered their lower selves, or baser attitudes and emotions, to a higher consciousness. They are dedicated, committed, loving and joyous entities who took the time and found the courage to go beyond all limitations, all dogmas scientific and religious. They fully accepted and loved self. They neither shrink with fear or anger at the judgments or condemnations of others, nor do they swell with pride from praise or adoration. The greatest masters will remind you that they are but a mirror of what is within you, for if it wasn't in self you could never recognize it.

They are a blessing to life and to all they come in contact with. There are great masters upon this plane, and what is done on the outskirts of their aura is incomprehensible. They are vibrational bridges or anchors of light. Because of them this plane is spared much of the chaos and confusion the collective consciousness of humanity has set into motion. There are those who, with a wave of their hand, could end any disaster or calamity, yet they know this would stunt the evolution of humanity. Their divine intervention has saved nations and the planet on many occasions. Although free will is honored, there is a limit to allowing.

To insure the continuation of evolution, they have altered the course of humanity on many occasions. They are your brothers; they are born of the original light as you are, yet they are fully realized. They know they are Gods and they have been babysitting you, so to speak, until you remember. They are not here to live your life or tell you what you should or should not do. They guide, clarify options and remove the clouds so that you can see better. They teach you that all you need to do is remember that all knowledge is within, and that you are the way. The purpose of a master is to remind you that you are the master. They are mirrors and examples of the light that lights every human, which is the light of God. They are your brothers and sisters. They are Gods and Goddesses. They are awake.

Rites, Rituals & Talismans

Rites and rituals are found in all civilizations. They are for the purpose of guiding and focusing the mind to create a desired effect. They provide a method for gaining a conviction. Many have become lost in their rites and rituals. They believe the only way they can receive the desired effect is by performing the rite or ritual.

Rites and rituals often include talismans. To some, the loss of a talisman used in a ritual will negate the effect of the ritual. The mere misplacement of a stone, feather or crystal, or the failure to perform the rite or ritual to perfection also negates the effect. Others believe that there are severe consequences for making a mistake in performing rites or rituals. These misunderstandings are all based upon a false belief that one must appease God to get the desired effect. Those who believe in severe consequences believe in a punishing God rather than a God of unconditional love. Rites, rituals and talismans have no power other than what you give them. It is the conviction and belief of the ones performing the rites and rituals or using the talismans that create the desired effect. In other words, it is all done within the mind.

What happens if you lose your talisman? If you believe it had power, you also lose your power. What happens if the rite or ritual was not performed satisfactorily? If you believe it had to be, you will also believe you are not worthy of the desired effect. It is as you believe. Only when you believe and have gained the necessary conviction will the magic happen. The magic is in the mind. You are the magician. Do not give your power away to rites, rituals and talismans. Remember that they are tools and that you are the power behind the tools.

Do they have a purpose? They do. When Gods gather together and their minds are united and guided, focusing on a desired effect, the power to manifest that desire is greatly magnified. If a talisman reminds you of your divinity and it brings you joy, keep it. When you gather, just remember it is the Gods who gather that create the experience. If you want to become a great God, all you need is a mind with great conviction.

There was a great magician who, one day, pulled out three ornately decorated boxes and told his apprentices to choose which box the magic was in. Each apprentice chose a box, and each was told he was wrong. The apprentices returned, after much discussion, and asked the magician which box had the magic in it. They believed one of them had to be right. The magician pointed to his head and said, "This box," while pointing to his head. "The magic is in the mind."

2

Earth Changes

Earth changes begin from a source unknown to most mainstream scientists, yet the mystics and oracles of old understand the cosmic cycles and manifesting force behind creation. In order to understand the mechanics and driving force behind Earth changes, one must understand the vibrational continuum.

As previously explained, consciousness lowers into light. Light carries with it consciousness. It then lowers itself to energy, which is also conscious, and then lowers to mass. Therefore, all mass has consc10usness.

The Sun is the first cause we are aware of as a creative driving force behind nature. There is a greater consciousness directing the Sun. In the ancient text it is written that the Sun is the life giver. It is what created the Earth and it regulates and sustains all life in this solar system. There is a feedback loop that connects the Earth and all life with the Sun.

The Sun has been expanding for quite some time. The coronal mass ejections and solar flares that the sun produces have been increasing exponentially. The Earth was created by a massive coronal mass ejection which found its cradle orbit and began to cool into a sphere over billions of years. The Earth then went through its evolutionary process like many other planets within the universe, including intervention from other advanced interstellar and interdimensional beings that were sometimes beneficial and other times destructive. Natural and manmade catastrophes due to the misuse of technology have plagued the Earth for millions of years. Through this process the Sun continued to sustain and regulate life as it does today.

Where would you be if the Sun did not rise to warm the planet and feed the plants and all other life that depend upon absorbing solar energy? To one degree or another, all life depends upon the Sun, and the Sun is now changing. The entire solar system is moving into a zone in the universe where there is more energy that is adding to the life-giving rays of the Sun. The energy in this system has increased exponentially. The amount of time it takes for the sun's rays to hit the Earth has increased over 300 percent during the past decade.

This information was known by past mystics and sages who documented solar cycles. The Mayan calendar, the Aztec calendar, the Vedas and other ancient teachings speak of these cosmic cycles, each having their own name for them. The procession of the equinoxes, along with other knowledge concerning greater cycles in our galaxy, was known millions of years ago and is written or built into ancient temples and pyramids. There are many prophecies concerning these times of change, written in sacred books of every culture, yet these events are not set in stone. They are an early warning system.

Native American prophecies talk of the white man returning. The prophecies are symbolic, and say that if the white man comes with the cross with the circle, welcome him for he has not forgotten the sacred circle of life. If he comes with the cross without the circle, dark days are ahead. These prophecies also detail the 'gourd of ashes' (the atomic bomb); the 'spider webs in the sky after which follows the plagues' (the chemtrails); the 'Tee Pee falling from the sky' (the deorbit of the Mir space station); the 'flipping of the sun' (the sun recently reversed its poles); and the 'great beast with a cloud 2,000 miles around' (a representation of the 2,000-year reign of destruction and tyranny). In the moment that this 2,000-year reign consumes itself-when it appears all hope is lost-there will be a transition and we will move into the thousand years of peace and a shift into the next world.

There are petroglyphs that show two snakes converging and eventually overlapping, representing the merging of the third and fourth dimension. During this process people will begin to see shadow people and have nonphysical and spiritual experiences as the veils begin to grow thin between the two worlds. They will see things in their peripheral vision yet when looking straight on, these things will disappear. This is due to the cones within the eye that are set up to see the other planes and dimension through peripheral vision. They will begin to see energy fields and auras as well. One of the most powerful petroglyphs shows two parallel lines representing two paths. One path is the path of the intellect and technology. The other represents the spirit, heart connection, living in harmony close to nature. Those living a spiritual natural life continue where the other path ends. This is a profound message concerning the days to come.

The mega solar cycle (otherwise called the shift of the ages) that we are now in will have unprecedented effects on humanity and the Earth. The effects of these Earth changes will continue to increase on all levels until the great shift into the next world or dimension.

On the Earth level, the increase in solar activity will create severe and erratic weather with wind speeds breaking all known records. Tornados and hurricanes, along with massive storms causing great flooding, will continue to escalate. There will also be changes in the jet streams that will bring rain to deserts and drought to forests. Earthquakes and volcanic eruptions will also increase exponentially as we move into what is called by many the 'end times.' The Earth is expanding as it absorbs more of these energies. The poles will melt down rapidly, sea levels will rise, oceans will shift as tectonic plates rise and fall and the Earth will take on a whole new topography.

On the human level, the coronal mass ejections and solar flares affect the bio-electric fields around the human body. This starts a process where all life is vibrationally lifted. There will be emotional outbursts, intense mood swings and leaps in consciousness during this process. Some will ride the waves to ecstatic states of consciousness and emotional well being. Others will project and blame as their unresolved issues, old wounds and traumas begin to surface. This will be seen in personal and business relationships; the political arena; the relationship between man/woman and the Earth; and the relationship between man/woman and God. All these relationships will be redefined.

The physical bodies of all life will be altered through DNA changes initiated by the Sun. Scientists have found those who practice deep meditation techniques or have had Near Death Experiences (NDEs) undergo a change in their DNA. More codons are activated, which will boost the immune system and bring greater mental clarity and overall better health and well being. The Sun is bringing this same gift to all life on Earth. Those who choose love, compassion and service to others will fare the best through these changes. Those who continue to exist in the separative consciousness of selfishness or disservice to humanity and the Earth will not fare well.

The lower vibrational attitudes and emotions such as fear, greed, jealousy, anger and 'againstness,' upon which the controllers operate, will not make it through this shift. They will do everything possible to shut down the evolutionary process and maintain the status quo, thus maintaining their controlling hold on humanity and the Earth. They will use every method possible: HAARP, psychotronics and chemtrails. Other technologies designed to shut down the vortexes will be employed. The enslavement through dependency, and the survival mode they have held you in for eons, will be apparent in the days to come.

Ask yourself, who is the enemy of the oil industry? Free energy: clean, earth-friendly energy, and such things as zero-point technology.

What is the enemy of the pharmaceutical and medical industry? Health and well being: the cure to illnesses. What is the enemy of the war industry? Universal peace. Look who is governing the planet. Is there any wonder why you do not have free energy, antigravity, the end of disease, and universal peace? Are you a willing participant, capitalizing at the expense of humanity and the Earth?

The actions of the tyrants will all be in vain, for this is a growth process that cannot be stopped. The age of tyranny is coming to a close. The only short-term gain experienced will have severe long-term consequences. Their bodies will fail, their institutions will crumble. When the Earth makes its transition, they will not make the shift and will end up on lesser planes or stuck in the void. This is a universal event-there is no place to hide, including the underground facilities. All life, all form is going through this shift. There will be incredible social and economic changes during this process, including personal relationships with lovers, family and friends. All that which does not align with love, compassion and service will cease.

It is the end of an age and the beginning of another. It is what is referred to as the thousand years of peace, yet at the end of every age there is a great purification, which is occurring now. The last purification cycle was water, the next is fire and the fire is the spirit, the consciousness behind the Sun, yet the sun will be the method of delivery and regulator in this solar system. There are grand entities that can and have intervened in this process. They are here to ensure evolution continues to go forward. They come from many levels, planes and dimensions. They are known as the greater family of humankind. They serve the creator within all creation and see humanity and the Earth as a part of creation that is in dire need of assistance. The current civilization is unsustainable, the environment is on the brink of collapse and they believe a civilization and a planet is a terrible thing to waste. They cannot interfere with free will, for they are bound by universal law.

The future is determined by several factors. There is the Earth and her destiny of cleansing and healing herself, thus continuing to provide a platform for life. There is the individual and collective consciousness. There is also divine intervention, but such intervention must be earned.

There must be changes in consciousness and action. There have been giant ships that have placed themselves between the Earth and the Sun to shield the Earth from enormous solar flares that would have ended this civilization. These ships have changed the nature of fault lines, relieving the pressure and settling down volcanoes in an effort to buy us time. It is a gift. Use it wisely.

Now is the time to choose. The choice will be the downward spiral into social, economic and environmental collapse: the downward spiral in which tyranny wishes to lead us. Their world is unsustainable. The other option is the upward spiral: choosing love, compassion and service to others, including all life and ultimately the restoration of nature back to its pristine beauty.

I would suggest the upward spiral-holding your political, religious and business leaders accountable to the universal principles necessary for a healthy society and environment. Universal peace, brother/ sisterly love, individual and collective freedom and prosperity, a strong reverence for life, and an honoring of the sacred circle of life are mandatory to ensure the continuation of humanity and the Earth.

3

Moving Onward

Money

Money is neither good nor evil. It is merely the accepted exchange of today's society. It is best to look upon money as energy directed by consciousness. This energy, money, can be directed selfishly, at the expense of humanity and nature, which results in only a temporary, short-term gain. Or it can be directed selflessly for the betterment of humanity and nature, which results in a continuous, everlasting, long-term gain. The best investment humanity can presently make is an investment in the healing and awakening of individual and collective consciousness. The destiny of the Earth is governed by the individual and collective consciousness of those who reside upon it.

Consciousness creates reality. When you invest in cleaning up your consciousness, you become a light to the world, assisting others in cleaning up their consciousness. What you have then is a forward movement back to Eden. Consciousness is the most valuable possession in the universe. It is a gift from God. It creates your tomorrow. There is no jewel, castle or amount of gold that is worth consciousness. Many have defiled their consciousness and have literally sold their souls whoring for money, security, status and a lifestyle or image having little or nothing to do with their true soul's desires. It is all for the dreams and images of others. They have given up everything that is truly of value. They have become so programmed by television and social consciousness that they have no idea what is valuable, what their purpose in life is, or what truly brings them joy. Many don't even know what joy is because the reference point is always outside of themselves. Their joy is based upon images, objects and outer appearances.

Did you know that all you have to do to sell something is to attach sex to it? A few scantily clothed bronzed men and painted women who will love you and accept you into their "in crowd" and ... Presto! The image and the desire are created. Few ask themselves, "Is it my soul's desire to experience or own that?" or "Is this my purpose in life?" What we are saying is that the better portion of humanity is constantly bombarded, hypnotized and programmed with these images, and kept off balance and out of touch with their purpose for being and their true soul desires. Priorities and values are, in most cases, backward.

The prime directive is to acquire the money to buy the products necessary to conform to a fashionable image. This image was given by those who sell the products. Wake up!

What most people are searching for is love and acceptance out there. What you don't realize is that when you love and accept yourself, you don't need all the props. What you are really searching for is feelings. Where do the feelings come from? Material objects do not possess feelings. They are merely touchstones. The feeling comes from within. People do not make you feel happy, loving or hateful; these emotions come from within. When you realize this, freedom is just around the corner. Your love, joy and happiness will no longer depend upon material acquisitions or others. It is hard to imagine being in love with love, being happy for no reason, or just plain being, without constantly seeking touchstones or people to make you happy.

Much of your greatest unhappiness is concerning the issue of money or the lack of it.

Love yourself enough to get to know and be with yourself, which means taking time away from your labor. There will be a shift in consciousness. Soon what you will desire is to experience real people who are in touch with themselves, their true selves. If you desire to experience your true self, the best place to do this is in nature-free from the judgments of your peers and the psychic turbulence and social consciousness of the city. Find yourself a great rock or majestic tree and ask yourself, "Why am I not happy? Where did I lose the ability to feel the love and joy within?" To be loving and joyous is your natural state.

Concerning the history of money, there are a few historical facts we would like to share with you. There have been many civilizations-some recorded, some unrecorded-that have collapsed due to their consciousness concerning the material. One in particular was known as Atlantis. There were different parties within the Atlantean society much like your Republican and Democratic parties. One party was focused primarily on pleasure, sense gratification, and living a lifestyle regardless of its effects to the planet. They also had elitist attitudes and were not beyond exploiting and dominating others to meet their desires. Their scientific endeavors followed the same direction as their consciousness. They were known as the Sons of Belia!.

The other party was known as the Law of One and they were more spiritual in nature. They honored each individual as a unique expression of God. Rather than dominate or exploit those who were not as fortunate, they endeavored to educate, empower and raise everyone to equal status. Their scientific endeavors were also a reflection of their consciousness, and nothing was created or implemented that would harm humanity or nature in any way. There were also a lot of fence sitters who had a foot in both camps.

Nonetheless, the Sons of Belia! were more aggressive and overpowered the Law of One in their lust for power. The class separation escalated, their scientists went unchecked, they continued to dominate and exploit nature and those who were less fortunate, despite the warnings and objections of those true to the Law of One. They even fought among themselves. There are great columns and stone buildings being discovered as deep as 6,000 feet beneath your oceans. One is off the coast of Peru, the other is near Easter Island. These are the remnants of their cities.

There are many factors or reoccurring themes which signal the beginning of the end of a civilization. The Romans had a huge military spread across their known world. They held an elitist attitude and were known for exploiting the people and the resources of weaker countries. They became obsessed with their material acquisitions, positions, titles and status. Their priorities and values shifted, and morally they declined to the point of decadence.

Another part of your more recent history is the French Revolution. The Aristocracy followed the same path as the Sons of Belia! and lost everything-including their heads. "Does any of this sound familiar? Are there any similarities to today's society?" Hopefully humanity will gain the wisdom from these experiences and not recreate the past. As far as the universe goes, the Earth is one of the few civilizations that uses money. Many advanced civilizations found that money without the proper consciousness often breeds greed, class separation, competition and conflict. In their system everyone is inspired to reach their greatest potential, fulfill their own unique soul's purpose, and always work in the highest and best good of their civilization. Their environment is also of the highest priority. Because of this they live abundantly, crime is very rare, and their resources are always directed towards improving their quality of life, individually and collectively. There is no competition, only constant refining and perfecting. They each share and build on the accomplishments and achievements of each other and all are honored evenly. By serving the whole they have realized that they are serving themselves and God.

They realize that life is a system of equally important and interconnected parts, all of which are part of a greater system. This greater system is the omnipresent life force. They live an abundant, fulfilling life in peace and freedom because they have the consciousness for it. They have conquered disease, and they live hundreds of years. They understand the universal principles, and they live by them.

They do not have prisons because there is no need. They honor free will, yet have advanced counseling and healing techniques. The occasional few who have unresolved issues or who experience confusion, stress or grief willingly seek the help they need. Although it is very rare, they sometimes have an extreme case in which an expulsion is necessary. In this worst case scenario an individual is expelled to another planet where they can live out their lives without harming others. They are provided for, and the conditions are not harsh because it is not a form of punishment. It is what is necessary to preserve the consciousness of the civilization, which all agree is the first priority. It is done with firm compassion.

They know that consciousness creates reality. Maintaining a collective consciousness free of lower vibrational attitudes and emotions is imperative to the continuation of their civilization. At one time in your distant past the Earth was used as a colony for this purpose. This does not imply that you are the descendents of undesirable criminals. The few expelled to the Earth did not survive as a colony.

These same advanced healing techniques are surfacing within your own civilization. The higher consciousness and energy is inspiring new ways and techniques to deal with the problems of society. Those who are acting selfishly, arrogantly and ignorantly are becoming increasingly unfashionable. Those who depend on outer appearances to establish self worth will be seen for their shallowness. Those who hoard and misuse their power or financial status and obtain their wealth at the expense of humanity or nature will be held in disgust rather than being admired.

There is a light coming on within their souls also, and they, too, are constantly reevaluating their lives. They wonder why they are not happy, why they cannot find love, why they are so insecure, and whether it is all worth it. Everyone wants to be loved and respected, and in their hearts, everyone truly desires that no one suffer. That is what resides within the hearts of all humanity, and that is what is coming forward.

There are universal laws concerning growth and abundance found in nature. It is natural for everything to grow not only in size but number. A small acorn can become a mighty oak tree. A kernel of corn will grow a stalk producing one or more ears of corn. Each ear of corn has within it five hundred or more kernels, each having the ability to grow a new stalk with more ears and thousands of more kernels.

Another universal law is the law of circulation. In nature everything is constantly circulating. As a plant draws carbon dioxide, water, minerals and fertilizer from the soil, it creates oxygen, food and shelter for the animals. The animals become food for other animals, produce manure to fertilize the land, create more carbon dioxide for the plants, and eventually, return to the land. Everything is in constant circulation.

If this system works and these universal laws apply to nature, why can't they be applied to society? If everything is growing, reproducing abundantly, and constantly circulating, why is there lack? Why can't humanity live under the same system? It is natural! How did we become so unnatural? What is blocking the circulation, the growth and abundance? Wake up, humanity! Who controls your monetary system? Who have you given your power to? Are they honest, trustworthy and of impeccable integrity? Do they love humanity and nature? Are they serving humanity and nature? Are they arrogant, ambitious and self-serving? Do they lust for money, power, and position at the expense of humanity and nature?

As the new higher consciousness and energy continues in the awakening and healing process, these questions will be answered. There will be no rock left unturned, everything will be exposed, and the reactions to actions against humanity and nature will manifest. History will repeat itself until the lesson is learned. The universal laws and a natural system based upon universal laws will come forward. It is destiny.

This brings us to another priority of great value, and that is nature. Those who are awake will find that a quiet, unspoiled sanctuary in nature is their grandest treasure. They will see the necessity of preserving nature, and they will realize that all those dreams and images given to them are usually at nature's expense. That is when their priorities and values are in order.

In the days to come you are going to have to learn to manifest the things you need, not the money to buy the things. You will have to reprogram your thinking. Learn to barter. Become less dependent upon money. You have no idea how enslaved you are to a piece of paper that somebody said was worth something-a value system that is not in your control. While the system lasts, make as much money as possible. Do it with integrity, not at the expense of humanity or nature, and use it to prepare for a time when there is no money. Prepare not only for yourself, but for your loved ones as well. Extend your families to include others. Invest in the healing and awakening of individual and collective consciousness, as well as the preservation, restoration and cleaning up of the Earth. Those are the two priorities of an awakened one. Both are necessary for the continuation of civilization as you know it.

The greatest and most valuable treasures in the universe are consciousness and life. These are the priorities of an enlightened one.

Fear, Security & Sanctuary

There is a great fear and insecurity within the hearts and minds of humanity. This insecurity is created by fear of the unknown, fear of an unknown future, and a gut feeling that something is headed your way-something ominous consisting of great change that will affect each and every one personally. There are those who know they cannot continue in their present jobs, their present relationships and their present consciousness.

There are also those who hear a voice within their souls reminding them of their actions against humanity and nature. Their greatest fear is the reaction. Many invest in elaborate security systems and surround themselves with guards, yet they never ask themselves why there are so many people out to get them. Politicians, government officials and the majority of the rich wonder why they have so many enemies, including those who would like to take a shot at them.

The only true security is to realize that we are not separate from God, humanity or nature. There is nothing more valuable than a gainfully employed individual who loves and admires those who made it possible. What better security exists than a world of happy, well-fed, whole and healthy people? What better security is there than living in a clean, wholesome environment with a balanced ecosystem? What better security is there than to be able to walk among those who love and admire you because you have been of service to them?

What better security is there than to have a consciousness filled with love, joy, peace and actions directed in service to and for the betterment of humanity and nature? Reason this the next time you feel insecure and ask yourself what you can do to create both inner and outer security. The next time you look at your balance sheet, think of the eternal balance sheet and the karmic debits you are setting into motion. There is no sanctuary or security system that will save you from the reactions to your actions, and you cannot hide from your consciousness that creates your tomorrow.

Computers & Intentions

There is a massive computer known as the "Beast," and the "Mark of the Beast" is the debit card. This will be the grandest misuse of technology and computers in the history of humanity. There is a group of clever individuals who govern the world economy. They have backed both sides of every war since the mid-1800s. They created the Internal Revenue Service to fund their wars. They control the Federal Reserve, which is a private institution. Just because it says federal does not mean it is owned by your government. The greater portion of the national debt, of which your taxes don't even cover the interest, is paid to them every year. They have been heavily involved in arms, drugs and other decadent behavior, the range and scope of which is beyond your wildest imagination. They are worth trillions and have held the better portion of humanity hostage for decades. Their latest endeavor is to have everyone on one massive computer. To do this they must collapse the economy and do away with world currencies. This way everyone will be on the debit card. The card will be governed by a series of computers that are in turn all governed by one massive computer, "The Beast." There will be a record of everything you buy, everywhere you go, etc. Your earnings will also be entered into the system. The questions you might ask yourself are the following:

• What happens when I give all my authority over to a computer governed by ambitious men whose lust for power at the expense of humanity and nature is insatiable?

• What happens when taxes, large government contracts given to their corporations and agencies, and a whole host of other charges are taken out of the better part of your earnings automatically, leaving you little or nothing for your labor?

• What happens when you become completely dependent upon the card for your food, clothing, transportation, shelter, etc.?

• What happens if they decide to take your card away because you no longer wish to play by their rules?

What these clever individuals do not understand is that when you try to rule or govern others, there is a grand loss of freedom. You yourself are governed by the next move of the ones you govern. How many must they govern and how much gold do they need to establish self worth? What they are really seeking is love, acceptance and security, yet they are going about it backwards. They are not loved and accepted for who they a r e - i t is what they possess. They are often surrounded by people who also want what they possess.

Some of these people will stop at nothing to get it, which includes so-called friends and lovers. This brings us back to security. Not only do they have to worry about their friends and lovers. There are a whole host of others who also desire a piece of the kingdom. What the international bankers have not taken into account is 1) the awakening and empowering of the masses that will not so easily be herded like ignorant cattle, 2) those within their own ranks who are regaining their integrity and turning around, and 3) an ominous force called nature that will put an end to their plans in a moment.

There are many other misuses of computers which will become blatantly obvious to you in the near future. Computers never forgive. They have no mercy or compassion and certainly know nothing of freedom or unconditional love. These are all attributes of a Christed master or the Christ consciousness.

There is no freedom in a rigid, mechanical society. Machines were never meant to run nor govern man, for within each human is a unique, creative, ever-expanding and changing God. There is a saying, "There are no perfect men, only perfect intentions." Many intentions do not turn out so grand. Mistakes are made. When mistakes are registered in a computer, there is no compassion, mercy or forgiveness.

There are many that believe that everyone should adhere to a systematic format, and that this format is usually created to benefit those who hold this belief, or to appease their fears. How can one create a format that allows each unique God to express according to his/her soul's desire? How can one create a law or system that covers all that is necessary to know, including the knowledge of all past life karma, to make an informed, just decision-a decision that may judge, condemn and punish someone? There is a greater system beyond the monkey mind, and the computers programmed by monkey minds are already at work.

Earth is an action/reaction world, known as the plane of demonstration, where unique and eternal Gods come to express. There are no victims, only self-created realities where all concerned gain wisdom from the experience. This is a system created by God, who

honors free will, the right to self-determination, freedom and elevation
into higher consciousness. It is not to be tampered with by fearful
monkey minds that desire to control and manipulate. It is also not to
be tampered with by the ambitious ones who desire to be the sovereign
rulers and lords of humanity.

Many have created an elaborate, computerized system, and they
have done this for several reasons. One is to control and enslave the
masses and another is because of fear of the future and change. Some
have done it for the sake of convenience.

This results in a loss of freedom and stifled creativity. Computers
can also stifle the ability to know all there is to know in the present
moment. The greatest computer ever known is omniscient mind, the
greatest internet ever created. Computers can become a dependency
and a crutch. Computers accept only what is fed into the computer as
truth, yet who feeds the computer, and isn't truth always evolving?
We must remain clear in our goals and intentions concerning the use
of computers. They can be a great asset or a great burden, depending
upon the consciousness that engages them.

There is another civilization that once had international bankers, a
war industry and those who equated self-worth to the number of people
they governed and who made their money at the expense of humanity
and nature. They governed by a massive computer, and there were
constant internal wars over who would control that computer. All of
these men desired to be the sovereign ruler. They were constantly
killing one another and taking over the positions of the ones they
killed. If they could not use character assassination, or public
humiliation, they used other extremes.

What they did not calculate was nature's reaction and the
awakening of courageous people who have had enough. They have
since evolved and learned a grand lesson in sovereignty, freedom and
the necessity for honoring and allowing each individual his privacy
and the divine right known as free will and self-determination.

Their computers are now used according to their change in
consciousness. Their computers can monitor the entire planet and send
high frequency healing energy wherever it is necessary. They can alter
time, distance and space, and even create or alter mass. There is one
thing they cannot and will not do and that is to interfere in personal
choice. They know one learns from experience, and they also know
that to interfere with self-created reality, individually or collectively,
would stunt the evolution of humanity.

This other civilization is watching humans follow the same course
they followed a long time ago, hoping that you don't have to

experience the pain and loss of freedom they did. They are loving, merciful and forgiving.

They will assist all those who choose these attributes as a way of life. Where are these brothers and sisters unseen? They are floating in your heavens in great crafts, awaiting an opening in consciousness. They are waiting for a conscious decision by humanity as a collective to end its destructive, warring nature, and to unite globally to choose peaceful coexistence with the rest of the universe.

Sacred Law

Sacred law and inner authority are what govern the lives of enlightened masters, as well as enlightened civilizations. Today's civilizations are governed by secular law and external authority. Understanding the differences between the two will be imperative to the advancement of humanity into the age of enlightenment.

Secular law and external authority are based on the premises that humanity is evil by nature, ignorant and incapable of governing themselves. Because of these fears and false beliefs, external authorities have been created which use judgment, condemnation and punishment as methods to enforce these secular laws. The rapid increases in crime, divorce and welfare recipients, and the ever-increasing burdens to enforce these secular laws using external authorities, are all testaments to the failure of secular law and external authority. Secular law and external authority perpetuate and escalate the very problems they were created to resolve.

Today's society is a grand reflection of law after law, enforcement agency after enforcement agency, and a bureaucratic nightmare of a system that is obviously a failure. Many will say, "What would happen if it wasn't there? There would be rape, murder, theft, etc." Is this not happening already on a grand scale? What have you got to lose? What has been going on legally within the system is another grand disservice to humanity and nature.

There is a saying, "The golden rule is: He who has the most gold, makes the rules." These rules are written to insure that those with the most gold keep it and acquire more of it, usually at the expense of nature and those with the lesser gold. Are not the laws of today written in favor of the rich who pay little or no taxes? Do we not have the best legal system money can buy? The great uneven dispersal of wealth is a by-product of bias, unjust, secular law, which is enforced by external authority. As the great uneven dispersal of wealth continues to escalate and the laws become even more restrictive, the enforcement agencies become larger and more oppressive and prisons fill to capacity. The burden to pay for these large oppressive enforcement agencies becomes heavier and heavier. The middle class and the infrastructure begin to collapse and soon their numbers are added to the poor. The riots begin and what follows is a grand revolution.

The rich, honorable and dishonorable throughout history become targeted in this process. Secular law and external authority has been the demise of many great civilizations. As it evolves there is a loss of freedom. Creativity becomes stifled, and class separation and abuses of power escalate until the inevitable collapse of the system occurs. So where's the gain? Many religious institutions use the same methods of judgment, condemnation and punishment to control and enslave the masses. Their secular law consists of rigid codes and doctrines, and their external authority consists of a wrathful God (that no man or woman can appease-living far away in the ethers), hell, and a devil to invoke fear, unworthiness and intimidate their flock into staying within the fold. It doesn't add up. Fear and unworthiness are the clouds that separate humans from God. Their God falls very short of omnipresence, and why would a loving father create a devil to torment his children and a hell of everlasting suffering?

Do you know the quickest way to create criminals? It is by taking the divinity out of the individuals and judging, condemning, and punishing them, telling them they are wretched sinners, restricting their freedom and placing heavier and heavier burdens upon them. This is what occurs as secular law and external authority evolve. Where is the love in that?

Do you know the quickest way to enslave the masses? Remove God from the individual, and tell them that only you and your institution have the word of God and that they must forsake their own inner guidance for your outer guidance. Did you know that tyrants have joined with religious leaders using these very same tactics in their lust for power and money? Have you ever wondered what a Holy War was, and how war can be holy? What are you warring against, other than the children of God in all their diversity? What happened to the commandment, "Thou shalt not kill"?

The last point we desire for you to contemplate is that whenever you give away your power to an external authority, there will always be those who will snatch it up, betray a trust, and use it for their own self interest. This includes governments, religious institutions and in some cases, friends and lovers. There will be a great polarity between those who wish to empower, and those who wish to control, manipulate and overpower. Power must return to each individual equally. All individuals must take the responsibility of governing themselves. Government must also consist of facilitators governed by consensus, and religions must lift and empower the individual into oneness with their own inner guidance and their own inner healer.

Sacred law is the law of love. It is that simple. Love God with all your heart, honor each individual as a unique expression of God, and behave as if the God in all life matters. Love must once again be the manifesting force behind all thought, all action, all creation. It is not that complicated.

The Codependent Victim/Savior Roles

The greatest disservice a savior can do is to save a victim from gaining the wisdom from their self-created realities. This creates devolution instead of evolution because one evolves through experience. When the experience is taken away, nothing is gained. In truth there are no victims, only eternal, powerful, manifesting Gods, walking through their own creations. Even children have their own agendas, along with a full overview of their lives before they choose to incarnate.

We live in an action/reaction world, known as the plane of demonstration, where consciousness creates reality. We magnetize people and events into our daily lives, according to our consciousness. Our attitudes, emotions and actions govern our destiny. How can there be victims in a world of self-created realities?

Did you know that when a victim fears being victimized and another desires to do the victimizing, and still another desires to be the savior, they all come together to co-create the drama? Victims also use their roles to manipulate saviors, unknowingly and sometimes habitually, into giving them either financial or emotional support. Saviors, on the other hand, believe they must earn the love and acceptance of the victim, by siding against the victim's enemy, and providing the emotional and financial support. The enemy is often another Savior who grew weary of being manipulated into giving any further financial and emotional support. Rather than saving, saviors support the victims in their roles, releasing them of any responsibility for the reality they create. Sound crazy? It is. A good portion of your law supports this behavior.

There are many saviors and victims vicariously working out their own unresolved issues and unhealed wounds through the legal and welfare systems. This has escalated into an unbearable burden, and the methods used by secular law and external authority have once again proven to be ineffective, only perpetuating and escalating the problem. So how do we end this madness? Victims must take responsibility for their self-created predicaments. They must be allowed to gain the wisdom from the experience. Educate them to take responsibility, stop blaming others, and move forward, healing the unresolved issues, wounds, patterns and false beliefs.

They must also stop manipulating others into giving them both financial and emotional support. The greatest disservice and insult to the powerful, manifesting God within a victim is to support him in his victim role. Saviors must learn to love and accept themselves and stop trying to earn the love and acceptance of victims by saving them. This includes those who make their living warring upon others for the sake of victims, or for their own self-aggrandizement. Saviors must also cease allowing victims to manipulate them into giving financial and emotional support.

Help is only help when one is taking responsibility for his self-created predicament, choosing to heal and gain the wisdom from the experience, and desiring to move forward. If the victim does not take responsibility, continues to externalize and blame others for his predicaments, and also refuses to heal and address the unresolved issues and false beliefs, any financial or emotional support will only reinforce, perpetuate and escalate the problem. The same powerful, manifesting God that drove them to their present situation can drive them out.

Taking responsibility for one's creations empowers one to put it in reverse. Both victims and saviors must become sovereign in their needs for love, acceptance and material needs as well. There is a unique, loving, joyous, powerful, manifesting God within everyone. Stop turning Gods into beggars. Rather than giving them fish, if they are physically able, teach them how to fish. Educate, heal the past, and provide opportunities for them to help themselves. Opportunities that are not just minimum wage, ones that are worth shooting for - jobs they can be proud of. The same God within you is within them also. Remind them of this. They are your brothers and sisters regardless of their predicament. Let us support this truth and end the codependent victim/savior role. We cannot afford to perpetuate it any longer, either individually or collectively as a nation.

Power

The ultimate power in the universe is unconditional love. It supports the universe, it permeates all, is all that is, and holds all that is together. It is the manifesting force behind all creation. This awesome power is within you. Within each individual resides a unique, loving, joyous, powerful, manifesting God, born of the original light, from which nothing was withheld. "The light that lights every man (and woman) is the light of God."

So, what's the problem? The problem is that original light is buried under layer upon layer of fear, guilt, unworthiness, superstitious dogma, religious dogma, scientific dogma and a whole host of misperceptions and wrong conclusions from past experience. You have given away your power to governments, religious institutions, lovers, family and friends and have settled for a much lesser identity.

How many of you can say, "I am God!"? Can you separate yourself from omnipresence? What did God create you out of, other than himself? If we told you that you have the power to manifest anything you desire, most of you would look at your present predicament and say either, "No way!" or "How?" The trick is to realize you have been doing it all along. Everything in your world has been manifested and magnetized to you according to your consciousness. That is how powerful you are. Some of you are a little slow. Some of you have been very creative in both directions. You have done nothing wrong. You manifest for the experience. When one realizes what they don't want, they can move forward and manifest what they do want. How would you ever know anything unless you experience it?

Power is one of the most misunderstood and misused energies upon this plane. Many have attached power to lofty positions and material acquisitions-usually gained at the expense of humanity and nature. To do this they must separate themselves into a lesser identity and an alter ego. The alter ego has separated itself from omnipresent God, which includes humanity and nature. In truth, any action against humanity or nature is an action against God and against the true self. Guilt creates the unworthiness that clouds your original light, and the inevitable reactions to your actions create fear and insecurity.

All this separates you from your power. Many carry out their entire lives this way. Another great truth to contemplate is: The only reason anyone has any power over you is because you want something from them. Be it love, acceptance or a material need. Whatever it is, it is a dependency. Love, acceptance and material needs can all be found within self or manifested from your center, which is a powerful manifesting God. These are tips to help you regain individual power. In the future, it will be necessary to be sovereign in love, acceptance and your material needs.

It is also important to assess just who you have given your power to. Whenever you place your power outside of self there will always be those who will snatch it up, often betraying a trust, and eventually use it against you. Where do the tyrants come from? They are created by the people who give them their power. Where did the international banking families and their political puppets get their power? You gave it to them little by little while you where asleep. Did you know Nikola Tesla gave you free energy and antigravity in the 1940s? In the 1930s, a pathologist named Royal Rife isolated the bacteria and viruses that cause all of your major diseases, including cancer, with a simple prism microscope. He also developed a way to broadcast a frequency that would destroy them within an eight-mile radius, eliminating the need for most drugs and major surgeries. Every human cell within the body is ten thousand times more resilient than the virus and bacteria cells, leaving them untouched during this process.

In giving away your power to external authorities you have also given away free energy and the end to most major diseases plaguing humanity. I will leave it up to you to figure out which special interest groups suppressed these devices and continue to do so. These energy and healing devices will resurface. There will be a grand revolution. It is already underway. Each individual must hold steadfast to his inspiration and find the self authority to act upon it.

The energy that is lifting and healing this plane will help you regain your power. This energy is empowering the individual, calling forward the unique, loving, joyous, powerful, manifesting God within. This will give you the self-authority necessary to reclaim your power.

Healing the Cause

All true and everlasting healing occurs when one addresses the cause. Treating the symptoms or physical manifestations of a disease brings comfort to the physical, but disease doesn't originate in the physical. The physical manifestation of a disease is merely the effect of a much deeper problem. Every disease originates with an attitude or emotion. Even genetic disorders originate from the attitudes and emotions of one's forefathers.

When you incarnate on this plane in a body, it is often a body of the same lineage you left in your passing. You enter a new body, but that body has a preordained destiny of its own. Not only do you have your own attitudes and emotions to contend with, you also have the attitudes and emotions stored in the cellular memory of your body.

In healing the cause, you must address the entire spectrum, which is timeless. There are past lives, cellular memories, trauma from the entry and birth processes, and traumas from age one to your present age. You can heal lower vibrational attitudes and emotions, wrong conclusions from past experiences, traumas within cellular memory and all other traumas.

Within each and every one of you is a great light, or consciousness, that once awakened, is lord over mass. It can heal the body in a moment, it can grow a new limb, it can even resurrect the dead if allowed. It is all determined by where one is in consciousness.

There have been many great masters upon this plane who have performed countless miracles to testify to what is being given here. So why aren't miracles an everyday thing, and why isn't everyone performing them? Because you have fallen asleep and been conditioned to believe the only way you can be healed is by a physician, a drug or something else outside of self. Did you know that belief is what constitutes a healing? There are hundreds of cures throughout many cultures for the same disease and they all work. Why? Because those who are cured believe in the method. The placebo effect is a grand example of administering a silver bullet. It usually consists of a sugar pill and a promise. Those who believe this "wonder drug" will heal them are healed. It even works for extreme heart conditions.

Humans were never meant to live for the body, subject to the body. The God who inhabits your body created it to be a servant, not a master. It is time to start talking to your body and to tell your body what you want. When one changes his attitude the body must follow suit. Whatever one holds within the mind will manifest. It is law. When one holds a picture of a robust, whole and healthy body, the body becomes the image. Your body is living in the past, so it must back up and start over with the new image. The speed and effectiveness of healing or change is directly related to your conviction.

It is one thing to believe this is possible. It is better to have conviction, to know this is possible, and to claim this possibility by commanding it forward from the God within. There are great masters who know this. They are indeed lords over mass. They know all diseases originate with attitudes and emotions. They are also not limited to time, distance and space, and can heal these attitudes and emotions no matter where they reside.

They also know that the body is constantly rejuvenating itself completely down to every last cell. One has only to remove the block or pattern, and the body will heal itself They also know how to create a quickening within the body by raising its vibration. How do they know and do all this? They merely woke up and remembered that they were Gods, lords over mass and born of the original light-the one consciousness that encompasses all consciousness.

The greatest master healer you will ever encounter is the master healer in you. All you have to do is change your attitude. All lower vibrational attitudes and emotions exist on the level of thought, and thought is the first cause of all that is. One can heal oneself by merely changing one's mind, and when one realizes there is only one mind in the universe, one can also heal others. Your physical body is only a physical example or hard copy of your emotional and mental body. When you clean up your attitudes and emotions, your physical body will follow suit.

You can also dissolve lower vibrational attitudes and emotions in others and in the race mind consciousness by focusing and sending out high vibrational thoughts-thoughts of love, peace, harmony, abundance and a whole and healthy body. The bottom line is that consciousness creates reality-and that includes your physical body.

There are many healing techniques designed to address these blocks and patterns, which are again lower vibrational attitudes, emotions and wrong conclusions from past experiences. Hypnotherapy, Reiki, various forms of process-oriented therapies, and breath and energy work all help to facilitate the healing process. Massage, acupuncture, acupressure and other forms of bodywork are also beneficial in moving things in the physical. There are also herbal, vitamin and glandular formulas which activate the body's own healing mechanisms.

We spoke earlier about the body being a physical manifestation of the mental and emotional body. The physical body in actuality is condensed consciousness. As the original expression of self, a whole and healthy eternal light being projects and lowers itself from consciousness to light, to energy, and eventually to mass, and becomes your physical expression. The original expression is distorted and blocked by lower vibrational attitudes, emotions and wrong conclusions from past experience. These inhibitors and wrong conclusions from the past exist within the mental and emotional bodies, as well as within the soul below the etheric self. The etheric self is a unique expression-a working duplicate of the original light.

In short, the body is a vehicle that houses a unique loving, joyous, powerful, manifesting God. It is designed to be a channel for and an expression of this higher consciousness and energy. It is not designed to be a channel for fear, unworthiness or any other lower vibrational attitudes and emotions. Holding onto and expressing lower vibrational attitudes and emotions creates a block or a pattern that restricts or inhibits the light and energy necessary to maintain a whole and healthy body. It is that simple.

Every cell in the body that has been placed in a stress-free environment by your scientists lives forever. Those who gaze upon cells with their microscopes observe that those who are in their joy have cells that are fully expanded and surrounded by light. Those who are in fear have contracted cells and the surrounding light is greatly diminished. This should tell you something.

The path to healing is to be a clear channel for, and expression of, the original expression, free of all lower vibrational attitudes and emotions, all fear, unworthiness and the wounds and wrong conclusions from past experience. This includes being free of religious and scientific dogma, as well as any other recycled ignorance and conditioning within consciousness that diminishes your light and blocks your ability to express as the unique, unconditionally loving, joyous, powerful, manifesting God that you are-your whole and healthy eternal self, the original cause. As you believe, so it is.

Brilliant Men & Wondrous Machines

This next understanding is very important because it is a key to the healing of your planet as well as your physical body. Antigravity, perpetual motion and magnetic generators that produce abundant, free energy have been given to humanity by several brilliant people. Tesla, Reich, Faraday and a host of others have come forward with inventions that generated and measured many forms of energy. This technology has been around since 1940. To have all of your transportation and energy needs met freely, efficiently and pollution free is the dream of many. However, that same dream is a nightmare to those who desire to control and manipulate the masses, keeping them under their yoke, plugged into and dependent upon their energy sources and products.

This technology has been labeled "TOP SECRET." The patents are all bought up, and those who would not play ball or sell the rights to their inventions were quickly done away with, "in the interest of national security." How secure is a nation dependent upon foreign oil? How secure is a nation governed by a family of international bankers who own refineries, wells and equipment and the transportation systems necessary to carry the oil? How secure is a nation dotted with nuclear reactors that are leaking time bombs that are poisoning generations to come, or an environment which is constantly being poisoned by petroleum products and emissions-emissions that are causing the holes in your ozone layer and the greenhouse effect?

Many of you cannot imagine a vehicle that would take you anywhere, at any time, for free. You cannot imagine all of your energy needs provided by a little magnetic generator, or batteries that store all that energy and last forever. Many of you are programmed to think this is impossible or fantasy, yet your government and some of your industries have the working models. They even have a few extraterrestrial examples of this technology gained from various crash sites (a whole book in itself). There are also radionic devices that work on higher frequencies or subtle levels that can eliminate agricultural pests, induce rapid plant growth, and heal the body. As we mentioned earlier in the 1930s a pathologist named Royal Rife developed a prism microscope capable of observing all bacteria and viruses, including the viruses which cause cancer. He also developed a process to destroy them using a frequency generator which healed and inoculated everyone within an eight-mile radius. It was cheap and simple.

Now, what would happen to the chemical companies if drugs, chemical fertilizers and pesticides were no longer necessary? You know those poisonous concoctions that contain powerful carcinogens which are responsible for the majority of your birth defects? Do you really think it is natural to have diseases and birth defects escalating on a grand scale? What if you could heal the body without drugs and surgery? Would you really need all those doctors and physicians with their American Medical Association (which has banned these healing devices)? Have you ever contemplated what would happen if you removed the cause of the majority of your diseases?

What do you say to a mother who is wailing over her newborn child with brain damage or deformed arms and legs? How do you tell her that her child is a by-product of herbicides or pesticides or unnecessary drugs and was a calculated, yet unnecessary, risk? What do you tell a boy whose favorite horse died a painful death due to an ulcerated stomach caused by herbicides sprayed upstream? What do you tell the hunter when he sees elk grazing in clear cuts on government land sprayed with the same chemicals? What do you tell the fisherman when his fish are ulcerated, deformed or belly up? How do you tell them it's their turn to taste the poison?

What kind of people would create these products and continually use them, knowing their side effects? What kind of people would purposely put a lid on clean technology that would free the people and create a clean, wholesome environment? What kind of people would allow this? We will tell you what kind. It is those who profit greatly at the expense of humanity and nature; those who lust for money and power: those puppets who are bought and paid for throughout the agencies; those who fear losing their jobs and therefore turn a blind eye to the injustices to humans and nature.

There are those who are lazy and do not want to be inconvenienced and those who don't want their tidy little world to change. There are also those who are asleep or hypnotized into believing and doing what they are told-you know, the walking dead. Your government, as well as most world governments, are run by big business and it is not good business to allow you to have freedom. If you are no longer dependent upon big business for all your needs, that is bad for business.

If government was truly your government, "of the people, by the people and for the people," it would surely make this technology available to the people. There is a grand conspiracy afoot, the scope and depth of which you cannot imagine. We love you enough to tell you this. We desire for you to survive as a civilization, and we are here to get you through an age. Clean technology must come forward. As a collective, you have power, and it's time to demand the free, abundant, wholesome life you so rightly deserve.

You are living on an abundant planet with abundant energy. It is all around you. There is wind, solar, magnetic and many other resources you are unaware of. The Earth itself is a giant, spinning generator. There are those who have tapped into these energies, harnessed them and can meet all of your needs abundantly and without pollution. There are also those who realize you yourself consist of energy and, when there exists an energy imbalance, you get sick. They have also found ways to balance your energy, keeping you away from the drugs and the knives. As we speak, there are prototypes of cars with electric motors whose batteries get over 300 miles to the charge. Imagine an electric engine hooked up to a magnetic, perpetual-motion driven electric generator with a range that is unlimited.

This is the tip of an iceberg of suppressed technology. How about releasing a little antigravity and perpetual motion? It does exist. It is powerful, efficient and nonpolluting. There is no reason to hoard this technology or energy. There is abundance for all. Nature planned it that way.

Forests

One of Earth's greatest treasures is the forest. Nowhere else in the universe is there such a diversity of life. Believe it or not, Earth is the only planet that has greenery, a yellow sun and an environment conducive to such diversity. That is why it is so precious not only to your civilization, but to others not known to you.

These other civilizations are your brothers and sisters. They cherish all life-even you, despite what you are doing to the planet. They have been throughout the universe, and they look upon your forests in awe for their beauty. They are very concerned about humanity's recklessness, greed and self-destructive behavior towards the very platform for life that sustains you. Where grand forests and majestic trees once stood there are now endless miles of naked, barren land. Forests that once covered major portions of the globe are now reduced to small dots here and there.

You planted a few trees to replace them, but what about the 100 or 200 years it takes to grow them? What about the 700- to 1000-year-old trees that were taken in their place? What about the extreme droughts and survival rate of these seedlings in light of the coming changes? They are left unsheltered, only to burn up in the summer and be washed away in the winter. How can you claim this to be renewable? You can create a sterile tree farm, the destiny of which is to succumb to disease and pestilence, but you can't create a forest with an intricate, balanced ecosystem necessary for a healthy continuous life.

Your beloved brothers in the sky wish they could end this madness, yet they know humanity must learn from the reactions to their actions. It's part of the evolutionary process. They watch as powerful carcinogens in pesticides and herbicides are sprayed on the highest peaks, knowing the waters end up at your faucets. They watch as foresters battle against the fires, pestilence and diseases they themselves set into motion. The foresters have never realized that what they are battling against is nature's healing process. They do not understand that when you remove the biomass and disrupt the intricate, interrelated, balanced ecosystem, you get weak spindly trees that actually emit a sound that calls to the pests. The pests finish off the trees to become the biomass for the next generation.

Even the fires are a natural element, yet because of the droughts brought about by man, they have become massive infernos out of control. Did you know a great portion of your rain is generated by the tropical rain forests that are also rapidly disappearing?

These are not acts of God punishing man-these are acts of ignorance by man. Nature is reacting, trying to heal herself. Acid rain and even the ozone depletion from burning fossil fuels, are conditions brought about by man. The beloved brothers watch as humanity, in ignorance, declares war in a collective assault upon the very platform of life that sustains it. They see no logic whatsoever in engaging in such self-destructive behavior.

The greatest diseases ever to plague Earth are unbridled greed and the false belief in separation from nature. These diseases, if unchecked, will cause an end to civilization. Those in power upon this plane depend upon the continuation of this madness. They will not tell you about the dying condition of the planet. They can't afford to. Those who work for them cannot see the ignorance in continuing the assault. They also can't afford to. The continuation of their paycheck demands that they turn a blind eye and a deaf ear to those who know. It also demands that they accept facts and figures given to them by those who profit greatly at the expense of humanity and nature. There is one thing they will listen to and see, for it is an awesome force about to deliver a powerful message that will affect everyone. It will shake the very ground beneath their feet. It is the voice of nature, the voice of God, which are one and the same.

If humanity could but see what those who watch from the heavens have seen throughout the years. If you could see a time-lapse film, made over the years of your planet and its forests, it would shock you to see the destruction, its rapid spread and the present condition of the planet. It would be quite obvious where Earth is destined if this continues and how little time is left to do something about it. It would also be clear why nature must intervene and stop this madness.

There is an example in your heavens of a planet where the unbridled greed of ambitious men, who lusted for money and power, went unchecked. They raped and poisoned the land, developed nuclear energy and eventually unleashed it upon their own people. Great canals, pyramids and gigantic stone faces are all that is left of a once great civilization. The example of which we speak is Mars-a barren, desolate planet where the game is over.

Parenting Masters

There is nothing more precious than a child. Angels sing when one of their dear ones is born on Earth. The gift of a child can be a most loving, joyous experience. It can also be one of the most complicated experiences the human adventure has to offer. Children are multidimensional beings with multidimensional problems. They can be better understood as multidimensional mirrors. They mirror their environment, and their environment is void of boundaries. They react to the attitudes and emotions of their parents, their immediate environment and other planes and dimensions.

At ages two to four, children are wide open and can see planes and dimensions most adults are unaware of. It is not uncommon to see a child pointing in the air and laughing or reacting in fear to what seems to be nothing. They can see angels, ascended masters, fairies and gnomes. They can also see grotesque thought forms, such as monsters and discarnate spirits in need of healing.

The best advice I can give those who wish to parent masters is to become masters. You have the sensitivity and the tools to discern and heal any situation. In reality, all children are masters and children today are aware of their divinity more than ever. They are here to experience the Golden Age, and many are ushering in and anchoring this understanding on this plane. That is their purpose, and many are fully aware of their chosen mission. It will be carried out in their own unique way.

This leads into a very important understanding concerning just to whom children belong. Children are not owned by their parents. They belong to God and themselves. They have chosen their parents for the experience their parents and their environment have to offer. Children are their own souls with their own purpose for being. They were before you were. In other words, you have been taking turns, often switching roles in the process known as reincarnation. Children are not here so that parents may live their lives vicariously through their children by controlling or manipulating them into completing the parent's own unfulfilled desires. Children have their own dream, or unique purpose for incarnating, and enlightened parents would do their best to discover just what that dream entails.

We cannot address the loving joyous side of rearing children without addressing the side that is often not so loving and joyous. There are ancient understandings that were as true in my day as they are today. Many of today's parents have thrown the baby out with the bath water in search of a more enlightened approach to raising children. A child needs boundaries. Without boundaries, children become dependent and insecure. A child also needs clear communication and clear choices. They need to know what kind of behavior is unacceptable and what the consequences of unacceptable behavior are.

It is up to parents to be fair and just and to decide "together" what is unacceptable and what the consequences of acting in such a way should be. Parents must be consistent and support each other once they have agreed. Children need to be guided to act lovingly, joyously, harmlessly and constructively, without trespassing on the rights of others. (This is a hint for those who are wondering what acceptable behavior is.)

Many of today's parents consider discipline a thing of the past and altogether not spiritual. Some people are overreacting to the rigidity and heavy handedness of their own parents. Some fear losing the love of their children. Others believe that discipline stifles expression and closes a child to spirit.

The first step to becoming an enlightened parent is to forgive your own parents. Until you have done this, your relationship with your spouse and your children will suffer. Look at all the things you dislike about your parents and see if they are also within self. See what may have happened in your parents' past to cause them to act the way they did. They, too, are products of their environment and have gained many false beliefs and wrong conclusions from their past experiences. Their parents probably had even more hang-ups than they did and passed them on as behavior patterns. Your parents had as much, or more, to overcome than you do because the collective consciousness of their time was very limited. This plane and its collective consciousness is constantly being lifted into a more unlimited understanding. They had much to overcome. Forgive them.

Another grand misnomer is the fear of losing the love of your children for disciplining them. Your children will love and respect you more as long as your methods are fair and just. A child will quickly lose respect for a parent with no self-authority and will continue to test them until they set some boundaries.

Even after boundaries are set, children will continually test them and will, in some cases, react violently until boundaries are enforced. The boundaries are necessary for their own security, for without them they become very insecure. In a child, you are dealing with an ego or personality that must be trained to allow the master to come through. There are some great masters, now on this plane, enslaved by an ego that has run amuck due to improper, or no, guidance. There are also those who, due to having no boundaries or discipline, have become tyrants trespassing on the rights of others. They never learned what behavior was acceptable and never experienced consequences of unacceptable behavior. They are now expressing violently, destructively and without any respect for themselves, humanity or nature. Many of them were rewarded for unacceptable behavior by acquiescing parents and are now continuing this behavior as adults.

It is not uncommon to see adults pout, throw tantrums and manipulate each other using the very same methods learned as a child. In many cases, unbridled greed, anger or any other lower vibrational attitudes and emotions in many cases have run rampant on this plane due to unchecked, undisciplined, unenlightened children continuing inappropriate behavior as adults.

Healing the child within the parent is a prerequisite for enlightened parenting. Your children will help you in this endeavor for they will mirror back to you all you need to know. They will press you into action. We spoke earlier about children being multidimensional mirrors. They are like little Geiger counters reacting to their environment. Their sensitivity creates a greater environment than most of their parents have, and they are affected by, and are more sensitive to, unseen influences.

Some of these influences are negative, and they create a negative response in the child. There are negative thought forms, limiting mental concepts and discarnate spirits. Often, the discarnate spirits include some of the child's own past lives. Lower vibrational attitudes and emotions (thought forms and limiting mental concepts) can come from parents, friends and even discarnate spirits. A child's environment, as we said earlier, can be filled with negative influences. This can all be healed by the parents. It is only a matter of loving yourself, calling upon the Ascended Master of your choice, and using the tools given at the back of this book.

As children become older and more objective, it would be wise to teach them the tools. It would also be wise to listen to them. They can often see what needs to be healed. This will help you to gain conviction. Doing healings also lifts the adult, putting her in a clear and peaceful environment. These are tips to help you restore peace and harmony not only within self, but within others also by removing the outer, negative, unseen influences.

A child must learn to attune to the higher vibrational attitudes and emotions of love, joy, peace, harmony, service and harmlessness. To do this, they must learn to direct their attention to the higher aspects of self. This takes self-control and self-discipline. It is up to parents to guide them and divert them from attuning to, or acting out, any lower vibrational attitudes and emotions. Guidance includes basic disciplinary action.

A child that cannot learn self-control is either out of control or under the control of something else. Like attracts like, and a child that is allowed to attune to negative attitudes, or express negatively, attracts negative thought forms and lower vibrational entities. Children become channels of what they attune to. Thus, it is imperative that they be taught to use their will to attune to higher attitudes and emotions, and to express lovingly, joyously and harmlessly, honoring the rights of others. All the spiritual healings in the world will not help one whose will it is to express negatively. You can remove the influences, but it must be the child's will to change, and there must be a conscious decision to do so. This is why it is imperative that the ego be guided and directed to express its higher nature as a child.

The greatest masters that walked this plane were born to parents who disciplined their children, ever guiding them onward and upward to fulfill their own unique purpose for being. They understood the necessity of self-control and self-discipline, and the pitfalls of allowing a child to run amuck without boundaries or a clear understanding of what is acceptable and what is not. At an early age they learned self-control and self-discipline, which made it possible to focus on, and surrender to, the God within them. A rebellious, undisciplined ego with no self-control is of no use to spirit or humanity.

Another point concerning the rearing of children is "smother love." This often creates a dependent child with expectations that are often unfulfilled later in life. Some parents hover over children, doing everything for them, allowing them no private time or alone time. These children often become very demanding, dependent and insecure. Children need alone time. They need to be challenged to figure some things out by themselves, and given the opportunity and responsibility to do some things on their own. This presses the brain to open and enhances creativity. It also makes them more independent and secure.

The next issue I would like to address is what to do when a child is not acting constructively, lovingly or joyously. Let us first address the tantrum. When a child is acting unreasonably, you cannot reason with him. You can, however, give him a clear choice either to discontinue his behavior and communicate with you, or to go to a place where he will not trespass on your rights or the rights of others to peace and harmony. If he chooses the first time to discontinue his tantrum, you have worked a miracle.

Should he choose to continue the tantrum (and most of them do), your next step is to remove him, or have him remove himself, to his room or another place that does not interfere with the rights of others. Acquiescing to his demands, in any way, is sure to bring you more and grander tantrums. This includes bribes for good behavior. At this point it would be wise to call upon the child's higher self and/or your own higher self and clear any unseen negative influences.

When the child is done with the tantrum and has gained control, communicate with him. Do not tell him he is bad. Tell him his behavior is unacceptable, why it is unacceptable and what is acceptable. Communication is very important and it is equally important not to condemn the child by telling him that he is bad or stupid. Address the behavior.

When do you begin to discipline children? Obviously not when they're babies. The only way a baby can make its needs known is by crying. As they get older, it is time to wean them of this behavior. A good rule of thumb as to when it is time to discipline a child is: If they are old enough to jump up and down and throw a tantrum, then they are old enough to discipline. The greatest of all challenges are the teenagers, otherwise known as the "system busters." They often question and rebel, which is natural. They are trying to establish their own identity, and it is a very awkward age.

They are no longer a boy or girl, yet they are neither a man nor woman. They want to be in charge of everything, yet they do not quite have the wisdom from experience. In Western society they often do not even know what it is to be a man or woman because there are no rites of passage. The archetypes given to them are often very unhealthy images, many of which dishonor one sex or the other. Many also do not have a clue as to what is expected of them as young adults. It is very important that these rites of passage be reinstated not with barbaric and painful rituals, but with love, understanding and compassion. Make a wonderful ceremony out of it.

There are universal principles that are not being taught in the home or in the schools. They are also mixed in with a lot of dogma and superstitious beliefs in many religious institutions. These universal principles and laws are necessary for a healthy civilization. The separation of church and state often keeps these principles from being taught. This is mainly because of the religious organizations wanting to add their images, codes and doctrines to the universal principles. They have nothing to do with religion and everything to do with life. The action/reaction principle, the laws of accountability and responsibility, the "interconnectedness" and strong reverence for all life, the principles of growth, abundance, balance, giving and receiving, equality, etc., are all necessary understandings for a healthy society. These need to be taught in the homes and in the schools.

Children are a precious gift, honored throughout the universe. They are your future. They are given to parents to guide and direct to fulfillment of the child's own unique soul's purpose for being. This purpose is always to express lovingly, joyously, abundantly and constructively, honoring the rights of others. To parents, I give my utmost respect and loving support in your undertaking of one of the most rewarding, loving, joyous and sometimes trying experiences this human adventure has to offer-the parenting of masters.

The Use of Drugs

I would like to begin this dissertation by telling you that I have not come to condemn or condone drugs. It is my desire to give information that will allow individuals to make an informed, conscious choice as to whether they will partake of drugs.

There are several reasons why one may choose to use drugs. One of the main reasons is the failure of today's society to bring love, joy and peace to the individual. Many use drugs to escape from an unfulfilled relationship or job. Alcohol, a joint, cocaine or heroin-they are all forms of escape. There are those who cannot find joy without a drug. Some people are very sensitive and are unable to shield themselves from the psychic turbulence of a hostile environment. In this instance, drugs are used to numb, or desensitize, as a means of protection. Another reason for using drugs is to have a spiritual experience and explore other planes and dimensions. A few choose drugs simply because it is fashionable and they are uninformed.

It would not be fair of me to ignore the fact that drugs indeed do have consequences. The short-term gain is not worth the long-term effect. Drugs can physically damage the body. The problems you seek to escape from are always there when you return. The highs you experience through drugs are a by-product of the death of your brain cells. Your brain is a receiver and the more one partakes of drugs, the more one damages his receiver and the ability to attune to the higher, more expanded consciousness (joy). The mind does not reside within the body. It takes a fully operational brain to receive the great mind of the great God that surrounds the body. Escape is not the answer. Facing your problems, healing them, or making the necessary adjustments to remove yourself from a situation that is taking you from your joy is far more productive.

As for using drugs for a spiritual experience, there are safe and natural techniques to attain the same goals. It is time for churches to expand and offer these techniques. They have been known in the East for over three thousand years. When one uses drugs for a spiritual experience, they are often blasted into realms where they cannot operate. They do not yet have the tools or the foundation. Can you imagine being filled with repressed fear, guilt or anger and entering a realm where your thoughts manifest instantly?

It could be a hellish experience-one over which you have no control because you are under the control of the drug. This information can be very disquieting for those of you who have partaken of drugs. It is not written to diminish your joy. It is written in love, to give you a true picture so that you can choose knowingly and fully informed. You are greatly loved, unconditionally, no matter what your choice. Those who have damaged their bodies can still open enough of the brain to become enlightened.

Mystery Schools

The mainstream schools of today base the greater portion of their curriculum on recycled ignorance. They do not inspire great, free-thinking minds. What they do inspire is conformity to limited mind. Children are programmed to compete, conform, obey and follow the rules and regulations of social consciousness-which is limited mind. They are not taught that they are creators of their destiny. They are not taught about the omnipresent, omniscient and omnipotent life force, of which they are a part. They are not taught about the great kinship of all life. They are not taught the principles of light or the divine science of manifestation and creation.

Children are searching for an identity. They are given the limitations passed down by teachers, generation after generation. They are taught how to compete, consume, conform, produce and live their lives subject to mass and the orders and edicts of others. Rather than teaching them that they are lords over mass, that consciousness creates reality and that within them resides a unique, loving, joyous, powerful manifesting God who cherishes life in all forms, they are instead taught about reactionary mind, subject to the world in which they live and those who control and manipulate it. They are molded, herded like cattle, infused and programmed with the attitudes and emotions of social consciousness.

Social consciousness is limited, reactionary mind. It is riddled with fear, unworthiness, confusion, limiting mental concepts, disease, false beliefs and wrong conclusions from past experience. When one projects a limiting mental concept or lower vibrational attitude or emotion into the outer world, it manifests and becomes a fact. In other words, it is real, tangible. It is then taught as a fact of life, yet it is only a manifestation of limited mind. Individually and collectively, humanity has been embracing lower vibrational attitudes and emotions, as well as limiting mental concepts and wrong conclusions from past experiences, and manifesting them in the outer world.

This is why the Mystery Schools are manifesting on your plane, Earth.

They are here to remind humanity that within them resides a unique, loving, joyous and powerful manifesting God. They are here to teach humanity that consciousness creates reality. Most importantly, they are here to awaken the forgotten Gods, dissolve the lower vibrational attitudes and emotions, heal their physical counterparts, and clean up the consciousness of this plane. They are here to establish the individual God, the Christ consciousness within each individual. They are also here to create a better world for future generations.

The only true and everlasting healing occurs from healing individual and collective consciousness, and humanity must take responsibility for this.

The mystery schools are here to teach you how. It is your choice as to when. In determining when, I would suggest taking a long, hard look at your present individual and collective consciousness, its physical manifestations and the future reactions. There is no time like the present. I highly recommend supporting these schools. They are a gift, and if accepted and allowed, they will change the course of humanity and the Earth (which are in dire need of redirection).

Monkey Mind

I wish to speak of a process that has enslaved humankind: the "monkey mind." It is consciousness run amuck, sometimes in endless circles, chasing its tail. It does not express in the moment. Rather, it builds cases against fictitious enemies, and it projects its fears and judgments into the outer world, avoiding responsibility for its own attitudes and emotions.

There are many processes within the monkey mind. We will address a few to help identify them. This will help you catch yourself, stop the process, and heal the attitudes and emotions without projecting them onto the outer world. Everything originates in mind. By bringing everything back into the mind, one can gain dominion over and heal any negative experience. To gain dominion over the world one must first gain dominion over the mind.

When you have a negative interaction with another person and, due to fear or unworthiness, you do not find the self-authority to express your feelings or take action, the negative experience becomes stuffed within self. The monkey mind then takes over. It goes back in time to build a case to justify the right to express. It also starts projecting ahead, and it sets up future events to add to the case. When the monkey mind has found sufficient grounds within self to express, it waits for an opening or event to unload.

The next time something happens that bears any resemblance whatsoever to your case, the flood gates open and a wave of unexpressed or repressed emotions engulf whatever or whomever triggered the response. Those caught in the wave are usually left dumbfounded, covered with the debris of a lifetime of your unexpressed fear, anger and resentment. They cannot for the life of them understand why a trivial (so it seemed to them) event or statement was met with such ferocity.

Unless the victim is a highly evolved being, his monkey mind will either start building a case in retaliation, or project it onto someone else. This creates an endless circle and perpetuates problems rather than healing them. Projecting our fears, anger or judgments onto the outer world creates just that - a fearful, angry, judgmental outer world.

Owning one's fears, anger, lower vibrational attitudes, emotions and wrong conclusions from past experience gives one the power to change and heal them. It is a matter of taking full responsibility for our attitudes, emotions and their physical counterparts.

Let me describe another trait of the monkey mind. When one finds his own life dull, boring or lacking purpose, his purpose becomes the lives of others. He measures others against his standards and images. When others do not meet those standards, he judges them and may condemn them or set out to fix them. God knows what would happen if he simply allowed them and got on with his own life.

Many of these fixers are, in reality, controllers and manipulators. Because of fear, they create boxes, standards and measures, and then try to jam unique Gods with unique destinies into their boxes. They also force unlimited Gods to conform to these standards and measures. Your present-day society is built by monkey minds. It stifles creativity and is stagnant and enslaving. Monkey minds that are seemingly "just trying to help" are quite perplexed when their loved ones rebel or lash out ferociously against all logic. It is because it is not logical to bind or constrict a creative, evolving, loving, joyous God.

Some have been very successful at imposing their will on others. The consequence is that they have given up their own life or unique purpose. They are busy living and controlling everyone else's lives. Those under their yoke have also become the walking dead, because the greater majority have also given up their own unique purpose and acquiesced to the will of another.

Your monkey mind has been programmed to be a consumer, to buy all that is fashionable for the reward of sex or prestige and eventually for your place of power, position and security. Sound familiar? How about a commercial that says, "The following message of silence is brought to you by the unique God within you. Take time to realize what truly brings you joy, what you want out of life, what your own unique purpose for incarnating is. This message will be free of all images, the desires of society, family and friends, and you do not have to follow any path or be anything other than yourself to have sex or gain the love and acceptance of God. This station fully supports you in following your own unique purpose. This commercial will play again and again to remind you to follow your bliss when all others demand that you take responsibility for theirs."

There is a station constantly transmitting this message. It is beyond the monkey mind. You must be still and quiet to hear it. All you have to do is turn your receiver to station C. H. R. I. S. T. 3200 FM, which stands for "Feel Me." It is constantly transmitting unconditional love, healing, and guidance from within.

A third aspect of the monkey mind is polarity thinking. Everything is either good or evil, rather than just being as it is. Did you know that everything is God and that without God, nothing exists? It is fear that demands judgment, and it is judgment that seemingly separates humans from God. It was the knowledge of good and evil, the "forbidden fruit," that caused man to first judge himself unworthy. Unworthiness led to guilt and fear. Consciousness creates reality. Duality thinking creates the duality world, the illusionary world of polarities. Everything 'is' and the 'is' is God. Before entering into duality or polarity thinking, tell yourself it is neither good nor evil, it just is. This will expand your consciousness and propel you forward into oneness with omnipresent, omnipotent and omniscient mind, God.

The fourth and last aspect of monkey mind we wish to address is your 'off' button. Whenever you are taken beyond your comfort zone, you turn off. Your brain shuts down. You may go on holiday and find yourself drifting off in a fantasy, an illusion, or a convenient image or distraction. This is your alter ego's way of staying in control.

Whenever something rattles your cage (a small cage at that, built by a fearful alter ego), you click off, switch channels and go somewhere else. Another time, another place, usually somewhere in the past. That is because the past is known and safe. Why not dare to enter the unknown? Explore a greater reality, a more expanded consciousness. If you really need to go somewhere, at least go forward. It is an inherent trait of the monkey mind to deny, discredit or attack anything that upsets its accepted reality, invokes, change or disrupts a lifestyle-even if that lifestyle is harmful to self, humanity or nature.

Rather than heed the words of prophets to change, humanity has found it simpler to chastise, discredit, ignore or kill the prophet. It has been done for eons.

It is wise to learn to stay focused and centered on love. Allow and take the messages of the prophets within. Meditate on them. Go beyond the monkey mind, and see if the messages are true for you.

To escape the monkey mind, one must monitor one's thoughts. Thought is cause. The mind is where all true and everlasting healing occurs. It is a matter of loving yourself, forgiving yourself and forgiving all the physical manifestations, as well as the people who were examples of what was within yourself. If one refuses to own his lower vibrational attitudes and emotions, as well as his physical manifestations, if he chooses to continue to project them into the outer world, and to blame events and people for self-created realities, he will remain powerless, and he will be a victim of circumstance.

There is a little monkey mind in everyone. Meditation, spiritual mind treatments and monitoring yourself will assist you in healing the lower vibrational attitudes and emotions and wrong conclusions from past experience.

The Monkey Trap

There is an ancient story concerning the monkey trap. A monkey trap is a coconut with two holes drilled in it. It is filled with rice and tethered down by a strap of leather tied to two stakes. The monkey sticks its hand into the hole and grabs a fistful of rice. Its fist is clenched so tightly around the rice, it cannot remove its hand from the coconut. Because of its greed and its fear of losing the rice, the monkey refuses to let go. The hunter comes and depending upon whether he desires food or to capture the monkey, he either nets it or kills it.

The greater portion of humanity is caught in the monkey trap. The hunter is nature in her endeavor to heal and cleanse herself. There are many who are holding tightly to their jobs, their positions, their homes and other real estate based in areas which are going to experience major upheavals.

There is a voice within people that is telling them to let go. This includes letting go of their fears, wounds, traumas and wrong conclusions from past experiences on both the mental and emotional levels. Because of the great fears of lack and an unknown future, they refuse to let go.

Love, joy, freedom and abundance come by just letting go of a lifestyle which, if evaluated with total honesty, many would have to admit diminishes their joy and freedom, and drains them of their very own life force. This lifestyle is killing the very platform for life upon which they carry out their dramas and fantasies. This lifestyle is coming to a close despite their wishes for it to continue.

Nature is not going to ask humanity's permission to heal herself. Lower vibrational attitudes and emotions are collapsing the magnetic fields in certain areas, and their human counterparts are raping the land and poisoning the air, water and earth. We are speaking of your major cities, especially on the east and west coasts. Those who cannot move from these areas are going to experience the hunter. They will first lose their freedom, and many will lose their lives. Eventually, they will lose everything.

Now is the time to take stock in your life, your environment and especially your geographic location. Look at what you are holding so tightly to. What is holding you back, keeping you from hearing the voice within and having the courage to do what you feel you must? It is time to get your priorities and values in order. Choose life! And when you move, behave as if the God in all life matters.

A change in consciousness is also in order so as not to recreate the necessity for another healing and cleansing. Preparation and healing must occur on all levels to continue into the coming age.

Soul Mates & Relationships

There was a split when the God seed that is you entered this plane of duality. Just as the Earth has two poles, so does humanity. Man is the positive, woman is the negative and both are equal. This is where the term soul mates originated. This does not imply that you are half God and split. Likewise, division does not imply separation or a loss of any of the attributes of the original light. The source still resides within you. It is only expressing as male or female in the physical embodiment.

You will realize that you can be unique and yet one, when you go beyond duality and polarities. Division does not mean a loss of anything. This should be a great relief to those who believe their destiny is to search endlessly for that illusive soul mate. Ascension and enlightenment is not dependent upon your other half. It would be wise to turn your attention inward and make God your soul mate. If you knew the odds of finding your soul mate and being in the right place at the right time, you would realize that turning inward is a much more productive path.

If you were to meet your soul mate and you had not cleaned house and rid yourself of most of your fears, lower vibrational attitudes and emotions, there would only be war. Your soul mate would mirror back to you the totality of self. Everything you don't like about yourself and the opposite sex would be reflected back to you along with any unhealed or unresolved issues.

This is why it is more productive to turn inward and clear the wounds, traumas and wrong conclusions from past experiences before you go searching for your soul mate. Another twist to the soul mate story is once you have met, no one else will do. You may find a comfort zone in another, yet it will lack the intensity and there will always be something missing. There may be no logical reason for you to have this relentless desire to be together, and there may be a million reasons why you shouldn't. When is love logical? It is a divine and holy love created by your very God-self wanting to unite with self. It is awesome, powerful, intense and sometimes a bit scary. It can ignite a flame of love beyond imagination and it can move mountains.

The closer you are to becoming one with the pure, unconditionally loving, joyous God within, the better chance you have of attracting your soul mate or someone of like mind. This brings us back to relationships. Each relationship is unique. For those who have ended a relationship, I will not tell you it will ever be the same, because it won't. It was a unique experience. However, I will tell you that you will love again, possibly the same person.

In order to experience a whole universe of uniqueness, you must let go of the past. It was a gift and it cannot be recreated, yet, believe it or not, there is always more. More love, more joy and another unique God to experience. Your eternal self has had millions of relationships, and odds are you will have millions more.

Clinging to the past and trying to recreate an experience by projecting the past on a new experience with a new, unique individual is not only an injustice to that individual, it is an injustice to yourself. You are separating yourself from all the new experiences life has to offer. When one is not appreciated for her own uniqueness, she often leaves. In order to experience the totality of any new relationship, there must be a letting go of the past, all preconceived ideas, all expectations and all the little boxes you created.

You both must be true to yourselves. When you come together, it must be as two unique, sovereign Gods. If there is a split, you must separate as two unique, sovereign Gods. Many partners are bound by fear-fear of losing favor in the eyes of God, fear of violating the enslaving human-made codes and doctrines of the church, fear of judgments of family and society, fear of lack, fear of loss of support, fear of being alone, or fears of many other kinds. Many are bound by 'shoulds' and guilt. These partners are not bound by love. They are bound by fear. They are so entangled with one another and are clinging so desperately to each other that they have forgotten self completely. If you were to look upon these relationships from another level, you would see so many psychic bonds and controlling, manipulating patterns, you would wonder how free will has any room to operate.

Whenever you acquiesce to the will of another, you diminish your light. Your soul is the source of your light. You must be free to find your divine purpose and follow your soul's desire-despite the whole of the world. If it is your divine purpose and your soul's desire to enter into a relationship, by all means do so, but stay in the moment. Do not spin webs or enter contractual agreements that enslave and bind you and your partner with future fears.

It may be your soul's desire to leave in the next moment. There are no accidents in the universe. People come together for various reasons. Some relationships are for the sole purpose of healing or fulfilling a commitment made on another level. When healing is accomplished or the commitment fulfilled, it is spiritually acceptable to move on to your next lesson or commitment. Limiting yourself to a relationship that diminishes your joy serves no purpose for you or the one you are with. What it does do is enable you to hold onto your fears, beliefs and limitations rather than addressing and healing them. You all have a right to love, joy and freedom, as well as the right to move in and out of relationships. We can no longer demand that others take responsibility for our attitudes, emotions or support. Within each man and woman lies a powerful manifesting God.

Another drama played out in relationships is the endless search for Mr. Right or Mrs. Right-you know, the one who is going to rescue you, solve all of your problems, or provide everything lacking within self. Many dive into one relationship after another with all of their projections and needs. When the infatuation is over and the curiosity is satisfied, what they are left with is self-the same incomplete self that was searching in the first place for love, acceptance and joy outside self. These individuals do not understand why they are unhappy and unfulfilled. They wonder what is wrong with the relationship. Rather than taking responsibility for their own consciousness that creates their reality, they instead blame their lover for their unhappiness-or move onto another lover, and another, and another. They cannot run from their consciousness. Until they deal with their own consciousness, they will recreate the same unhappy experiences. It will just be another face, another place, another time.

Many of these experiences are replicas of childhood experiences. A lot of inner child healing work is presently underway. Many are looking for a relationship with their father or mother in a new partner.

These relationships are for the purpose of healing the past. One attracts a person with the same patterns that wounded them as a child. Ideally, the childhood experience is recreated, allowing the person an opportunity to heal old wounds. However, many become victims and fall into blame, rather than healing their own consciousness and self-created reality. Thus, the experience will only be recreated later in life, over and over again until it is healed.

In dealing with these issues, whether they are abuse, abandonment or some other experience, it is wise to see yourself as a billionaire looking at a penny. Many spend their entire lives grieving over a lost penny when they are indeed billionaires. Although a wound must be addressed and healed, it is a very small part in a grand play that has gone on since eternity. You need not give it so much power or attention. Allow a grander Self to heal and have dominion over the situation.

One of the greatest of all tips we can offer concerning relationships is to establish an intimate relationship with your own God self before trying to establish one with others. This will carry you through the trials and tribulations of any relationship, as well as allow you to love others unconditionally on a much grander scale. It will also allow you to bond because it is your soul's desire and not because you are needy, insecure or programmed by society or alter ego.

Your God self's love and acceptance is steadfast, unconditional and beyond measure. It is something you can always depend on-especially when others are unloving or anticipating.

Your God self will carry you through the acceleration and the vibrational lifting and healing processes concerning relationships. All unresolved issues and inequalities in relationships and in society will come forward to be resolved and healed. The lifting will come in cycles and will increase in intensity. Each individual will have a choice. On the one side is fear: projecting, blaming, controlling and manipulating. On the other side is unconditional love and allowing. Higher consciousness and energy is lifting and empowering each individual to fulfill his own unique purpose for being.

Commit to love. Make love your lover. Commit to your own healing process. Commit to supporting others in their healing process. Most of all, commit to your own God self and your own soul's purpose for being. And in doing so, perhaps you will draw to yourself someone of like mind. Unite in freedom. Know the unique God within your partner as well as yourself. And give free will a little room to operate. Be together because you want to, because it is your soul's desire, because it brings you joy.

Just Friends

I wish to bring an understanding to humanity. It is from a civilization that overcame its aggressive, competitive and warring behavior by making a collective agreement to never go beneath the level of friendship. Before entering any relationship they agree to always be friends. If it is the soul's desire of an individual to move apart or explore another reality, it is discussed openly and honestly.

In the civilization of which I speak, the most honored relationship is friendship. If, between individuals, a mutual desire to explore a more intimate relationship exists, it is done with the understanding that they will always come back to being friends. This is also done in business relationships. In a business venture, decisions made are always in the highest and best interest of all concerned-including the whole of life. Each player is aware of exactly what is expected from him.

If the soul's desire of an individual is to change jobs or partners, there is a network that allows this to happen. It happens smoothly, with the blessings of all concerned. These people are not enslaved by their jobs or their relationships. They live abundant lives where each individual is doing what brings her joy. They are sovereign, honest and of the utmost integrity. They are not bound by the societal and religious limitations and moral judgments found on your plane. They are not controlled or manipulated into continuing in jobs or relationships that have lost their flavor. Their decisions are not made under the fear of loss or penalty. They have mastered their insecurities. All decisions are based on love.

Children are one of their most cherished possessions, and they are always taken care of. Their system provides for children. Each child is the child of the civilization. Parents are beyond the beliefs of duality and separation. They do not own their children. They understand that there is truly one Father and one Mother in the Universe and that they are expressing as an aspect of the Father-Mother God. Children are free to explore many fathers and many mothers, and they are more secure for it.

Now, I wish to answer a few questions.... Do they bond together for a lifetime? They do. Do they separate when it is their souls' desire? They do. Do they love and cherish their children? They do. Are they beyond jealousy? They are. They realize a soul is owned by God and by itself.

Do others also raise their children? They do. Do the children suffer from the diversity of parents? They don't, for it is accepted by society, and children are even more secure because there is never a separation. The new relationship honors the old, and everyone remains friends. It is not a burden to accept children into your lives-it is an honor. The new parent always is grateful for the gift of the former parent, though the child is never owned. Parents are always free to be with their children, and the details are always worked out graciously, to the highest and best good of all concerned.

The civilization of which I speak is of the same seed as humanity. They are a little further along in their evolution, yet it is the destiny of humanity to follow in their footsteps. They are a civilization of honest and sincere people of the highest integrity. They have enjoyed a peaceful, harmonious existence for thousands of years, and they are free to this day to follow their hearts' desires. They have prospered and advanced spiritually and technologically to become what humanity can only dream of, yet everything begins with a dream. There is one thing you can always depend upon. They will always be your friends. They have learned that to stifle or constrict a loving, joyous God who is ever seeking new and unique ways of expressing is to kill them. Because of their nature, they live to an average age of eight hundred years. Why? Because they truly live life as a loving, joyous and bold adventure, and they are free and supported in doing so.

Love & Forgiveness

One of the most powerful sayings of all time is, "Father, forgive them, for they know not what they do." Another rendition of this saying is, "Father, forgive them, for they do not know who they are, who you are, or what God is."

There is a lot of talk about dysfunctional families, yet let us expand our understanding to encompass a dysfunctional planet. If your world is not honoring each individual as a unique expression of God, and if your world does not behave as if the God in all life matters, it is dysfunctional. If everyone knew they were a God, residing among other Gods, and that God in its most unlimited understanding is pure unconditional love and joy residing within the totality of life, imagine what this plane would become. It is the destiny of this plane to return to Eden and to lift into the Christ vibration, yet between now and then, you have a lot of forgiving to do.

Most humans are no longer a reflection of the loving, joyous, powerful manifesting God or of the true image in which they were created. There are very few examples, or mirrors, of this truth. Humanity has strayed greatly from this truth, due to fear, unworthiness and wrong conclusions from past experience. The discrepancy differs with the individual and is directly proportional to the environments they have experienced. The environments and experiences are not limited to one lifetime, one planet, one plane or one dimension. It is the totality of all experience that creates the consciousness of the individual.

All experience is recorded in the soul as feelings. These feelings are often unconsciously acted upon. Fear, ignorance and wrong conclusions from past experience often govern the actions of many from deeper levels within self, unaware to their conscious minds. They truly do not know what they do or why they do it. They have become wounded and confused by negative experience. Some experiences have settled into the soul as wisdom. They are finished business, because the individual has gained the right conclusion from the experience.

Healing comes through understanding. Understanding allows one to forgive, release and no longer be affected by negative experiences. There is an omnipresent, omnipotent and omniscient being within everyone.

It can call the body forward to the whole and healthy now. It can dissolve fear, unworthiness and all lower vibrational attitudes, emotions and wrong conclusions from past experience. It can reinstate you as the whole and healthy, immaculate, loving, joyous God-the true image and likeness in which you were created. The first step is desire. You have to want it. The second is to realize that you are not who you think you are. When this is done, you will also realize that everyone else is not who you think they are.

Behind every mask lies a loving, joyous and powerful manifesting God-no matter what you think is real or what you have based your judgments on. No matter what fantasy or drama is unfolding before your eyes, behind every mask is God. They may not know they are God, yet is it not time to remind them? Is it not time to awaken to the fact that you are indeed Gods? Awaken from the dream. Is it not time to step out of the dramas and fantasies and remember?

Forgive yourself for forgetting and not seeing beyond the mask. Forgive yourself for falsely identifying with the dramas and fantasies. Forgive your parents, friends and families for forgetting who they truly are and for getting caught up and lost in the dream. Forgive them for not acknowledging who you truly are and for not being the mirror of the God within you. Forgive the overzealous men and their idols, who truly believe they are serving God. Forgive the world for forgetting, for not acknowledging and mirroring the fact that you are indeed God. Keep forgiving until you are empty of all fear, anger, blame, guilt, sadness, judgment, condemnation, separation and need for revenge.

Have compassion for all those who have become wounded and confused on their journey through life. No longer allow yourself to be fooled by the masks-yours or theirs. Awaken and remember your origin: a loving, joyous, powerful, manifesting God born of the original light from which nothing was withheld. It would also be wise to forgive God-who loved you unconditionally throughout all of your chosen dramas and fantasies. It is a God who has never abandoned you, but allowed you, honoring a divine gift called free will, and is a God to be found within you, all around you, wherever there is life.

A Note to the Atheist

I wish to impart to you a blessing, regardless of your truth. You are loved unconditionally, for love is the life force that allows you to be.

If I had chosen your path in my expression as Ezekiel, I would have had much less to unlearn. My soul's desire was to live in the forest and find God through nature. Unfortunately, I allowed myself to be ensnared by the teachings of unenlightened men. Do not judge yourself for not accepting the graven images of others. Man has created God in his image. That is why there are so many images, codes, doctrines and rituals belonging to these images.

It is a wise choice not to become ensnared in the confusion and the many images of men. It is unwise to continue to separate yourself from a God who truly loves you unconditionally. The pure unconditional love and joy of the Father resides within you. Only there is it to be found. There are pearls in all teachings. Let love, joy and unity be your tools for discernment. Disregard the shells of ignorance. You will never find the pearl until you crack the shell. I have seen more unconditional love and compassion in the atheist than in those who profess to be spiritual.

When one adheres to a rigid code or doctrine, one has a proclivity to judge and condemn those who do not. This love is conditional and limited, for it cannot love or allow anything outside of its discipline. This is a trap. Be thankful if you have avoided it. Love yourself as you are loved by the Father, and allow others their truths. In doing so you will become the example.

It is loving God with all your heart that opens the door to oneness with the totality of life. In doing so, the love of God will flow through you to the rest of the world. This is a simple truth that humans have complicated. Whether you love God or not, you are greatly loved, yet you and only you can open the door. There are no conditions, no codes, no prerequisites. There is only love. That, dear brothers and sisters, is an infinite, ongoing truth-despite what humans have made of it.

Right to Joy

You all have the right to joy. You have the right to live the most loving, joyous, abundant life imaginable. If anyone tells you differently, they are enslavers. They are trespassing on your divine right to free will and self-determination. The only thing you should do is that which brings you joy. God is bliss, and when you are following your bliss, you are following God. All that God asks of you is that you be happy. The unconditional love of God supports you in whatever makes you happy.

A question seldom asked is, "Why am I not happy?" It would also be wise to ask "What do I truly want? What is my innermost desire?" The most empowering thing to do is to find the courage to live your soul's desire despite the whole of the world. The best contribution anyone can make is to live a thoroughly happy and joyous life. Become an example of that life, so that others may follow your lead. Do not look to others for acceptance or approval. Accept and approve of yourself. God has accepted you and approves of you, for the love of God is unconditional. Is that not enough? You are always okay with God. You can use that as your mantra when you are not okay with others. Your innermost desires are God's desires, and God is love.

God is also freedom. It is not God's plan that you live your life for others. Following your bliss will include others, yet do not become enslaved by the "shoulds" of family, or society or by another's picture of reality. You have been told what you should be, what you should do, what you should wear, what you should eat, and when you should do all of these things. Has anyone told you that you should do what makes you happy, and then supported you totally in that role? I am and I will, for I love you as God loves you. Dispense with the "shoulds" and "have to's." Take the time to find yourself. Get in touch with your innermost desires, and find the courage to live them. Be happy, and be a blessing to life.

Simplicity

We cannot expound enough upon the benefits of simplicity. Have you ever wondered why simple people often have glowing eyes and beautiful smiles? Some of the most impoverished people experience more joy than those with the greatest of kingdoms. Have you ever wondered what their secret is? It is quite simple. They realize that material objects possess no joy. They also realize that joy is an inward experience, and they do not look for their joy in the transitory, ever-changing outer world. Their kingdom, love and joy are within-changeless and safe from an ever-changing outer world. They have not been hypnotized by the "American Dream," and though many own material objects, they are not owned by the objects. Their self-worth is independent of their material acquisitions in the outer world. Their love, joy and self-worth are changeless, operational, intact and within. That is why they have glowing eyes and beautiful smiles.

4

Fantasies, Fables & Parables

The Trapping of Angels

In a time before time, there was an angel named Poseffini. She was a manifestation of pure love and joy. She was as free as the wind, and she followed her joy wherever it led. She never realized the joy was within her. Whoever came within her aura was filled with love and joy. They would often do a little dance, a kind deed or hug the closest friend. Often one would see someone hugging a tree in her presence. Many could not perceive her, yet her presence would cause them to do the oddest things.

All Poseffini saw was the love and joy reflected back to her by all that she experienced. She lived in a realm of light with a myriad of other forms expressing in light bodies. It was a realm where dreams manifest instantly. It was far from boring, for they would interact with each other's dreams. There was always something to do.

The Spirit of the Moon delighted in Poseffini's adventures. She would often send a moonbeam for Poseffini to ride on to other planes and dimensions. She brought her love and joy to far away places many have not even dreamed of.

Poseffini was grateful for all her adventures, and she wanted to express her gratitude to whomever was sending the wonderful beams that guided her. That thought alone created the manifestation of Poseffini standing in front of a beautiful woman with long silken robes. The beautiful woman was of spirit. The stars could be seen through her as she drifted in the heavens. Poseffini was overwhelmed by the beauty and grace of the Spirit of the Moon, as well as by the love and joy emanating from her being. Poseffini had never felt such a nurturing essence.

The Spirit spoke in a warm and gentle voice, "Poseffini, my dearest Poseffini, you have brought me so much joy. I have been with you in all your adventures. I have also shared in the love and joy you brought to others. What you have not realized is that the love and joy you experience is the universe reflecting back to you your own love and joy. You came to thank me for your adventures, yet it is I who wish to thank you for sharing them with me. I wish for you to think of me as your equal. Do not place me above yourself, for that only diminishes your own light. What you see in me is within you, for you could not recognize it if it wasn't within self. I wish for you to see me as a friend to share in your love and light."

This dissolved all barriers between Poseffini and the Spirit of the Moon. They spent hours, which were months, even years, in other dimensions, reminiscing about adventures and experiences they had shared. This created a bond of familiarity that would always be with them. Poseffini asked the Spirit about a planet she passed on the way to the moon. It was emerald green and looked enticing. Poseffini saw sadness in the face of the Spirit of the Moon. The Spirit paused for a few moments and spoke, "The planet you passed is known as Earth. It is the plane of demonstration. It is where an angel goes to experience mass, the lowest vibration of God. To understand the totality of God, one must experience this plane. Unfortunately, many have become entrapped by it."

Poseffini didn't understand. She wondered how mass could entrap a spirit. She could flow right through mass, and it would be impossible for anything to hold her against her will. The Spirit spoke, "In order to experience mass, a spirit must choose to become flesh. This is where the entrapment occurs. The physical body is equipped with five senses, and it vibrates at the same level as mass. Without it you could not truly experience mass, for you would flow right through it. As spirit you can see and feel the emanations of mass, yet you cannot hold it in your arms, touch it, smell it or hear it.

"Spirit communicates through thought and, though spirit can see, it cannot truly experience creation on the level of mass without a physical body equipped with the five senses-a body of the same vibration as mass.

"The physical body is rich in cellular memory. It has stored in its cells generations of experiences that were embraced emotionally. This is what allows it to adapt to its environment and evolve, making any necessary adjustments to continue. Recorded within the body is fear and pain. When an angel enters a physical body, emotions stored in the body become intermixed with the angel's own emotions. This lowers an angel's vibration. Even when the body dies, the spirit often carries with it the lower vibrational attitudes and emotions. This ties the spirit to the Earth and keeps it on the wheel of life, to be born again and again."

Poseffini was confused. She didn't understand fear and pain because she had never experienced them. Then the Spirit spoke of death, she was really thrown for a loop. She didn't understand how consciousness or light could die. The Spirit felt her confusion and spoke, "Poseffini, fear and pain are emotions that were necessary for the physical body to continue. Fear came from pain. Pain was a feeling necessary to bring attention to an area of the body that had been injured. Pain was a great teacher. It often saved the body from injury. Fear and pain kept the body out of harm's way. Pain in the belly often kept a body from poisoning itself. Fear of pain was the first fear. Humanity has been very creative with fear, and now fear has a myriad of forms.

"As for death, you are right in your understanding of the nature of spirit. Spirit never dies. Many on Earth identify with the body. When the body is no longer able to function, the spirit removes itself This brings grief and sadness to those it leaves behind, who still identify with the body as the identity of the loved one. The spirit is usually observing this in a light body, yet it cannot console those who are grieving, for it cannot be seen. Spirit can be felt, but those left behind are too busy feeling grief and sadness. Even the physical body never dies. It is composed of atoms. The very atom itself has life, and when the spirit leaves the body, the atoms merely disperse. Spirit is and always will be. What many grieve over is a picture painted by a spirit that chose to inhabit it. If those in mourning would send a ray of love and joy to the spirit that left the painting, that spirit would feel their presence and know they are all right.

"I feel your next question. How does Spirit forget? To enter a physical body, spirit merges with the light of one of the parents. The spirit often chooses someone they are familiar with. When the child is born, the spirit enters the body. This can happen at birth or even months later. Upon entering the body, the spirit forgets its identity. It takes on a 'personality' that is a combination of the spirit and memory stored within the body. The personality is not conscious of its past, yet the past is still within it, stored as feelings."

Poseffini then understood how angels are entrapped, but she still lacked the experience to give her a complete understanding. Curiosity was the driving force that guided her into all of her adventures. At this point, Poseffini was fearless, for she had no reason to fear anything. After hearing the story of Earth, she was compelled to experience that plane and all it had to offer. She knew the power of love and joy, and that they would never abandon her.

The Spirit, being one with her thoughts, spoke, "My dearest Poseffini, I feel your desire. Your love, joy and freedom of spirit is in great need on Earth. You will forget who you are upon entering the body, but I will remind you when it is time. I will watch over you and be one with you in all that you do. You will touch many and cause them to feel the presence of their own guiding light. The angels have never been alone in their adventures. They have only forgotten and chosen the dream of separation. You will be a reminder and a blessing.

"There is one thing you must know before you go. There are those who will be offended by your free spirit, as well as your love and joy. You will remind them of everything they have forgotten. Rather than having the courage to change and join you, they will try to change you. Do not accept their way. Stay in the heart, and let love be your guide in all that you do. Most important, follow your joy. They need this example. You are one of many who have chosen to bring them this message. Our bond is strong, for we have shared so many joyous memories. I will always be a loving, joyous thought away."

Poseffini was engulfed by a brilliant light, and her next vision was of her parents. They were beaming with love and had tears in their eyes. She then knew why so many come to the Earth plane. If the love and joy brought to parents was the only experience, it was worth it. The first thing Poseffini learned was that people cry when they are happy. She faintly remembered the conversation with the Spirit of the Moon. She wondered how she knew so much about this plane. She heard the gentle voice once again, saying, "I walked this plane just as you, and I transcended it by loving it-all of it."

Favor & Worthiness

After losing a battle for life against an angry sea, a man drowned and found himself ascending through a tunnel of light, settling into a golden realm of light. The love, joy, security and overwhelming bliss were beyond words. He was in the arms of the Father. Feeling the love and joy of the Father, he asked, "How can I stay?" The Father said, "Whether or not you stay is up to you. I have neither told one of my children when to come home, nor have I told them they must do this or that beforehand." The man, still programmed from earlier religious beliefs, again asked, "What can I do to earn the right to stay?" The Father answered, "You are loved unconditionally; you cannot earn what is given freely and unconditionally. It is your birthright to use your free will and choose whether or not you wish to stay. You are always loved and welcome in my house." The man continued to bathe in the pure joy of the golden light floating in his own light body. After a little while, he felt the need to repay the Father for the wonderful gift of being able to experience such love and joy.

He then asked the Father, "How can I serve? What can I do to repay you for this wonderful gift you are sharing with me?" There was a long pause, and then the Father answered, "Whether you desire to assist humankind or not, you are loved and have a place with me. What do you desire? What brings you the most joy at this moment?"

The man replied, "I would not feel right within my being if I did not help humankind know the true nature of God. There are so many false and superstitious images. I want them to know and feel pure unconditional love, joy, peace and security as I have known and felt. As you are my Father, they are my brothers and sisters. We are all one. I now understand the meaning of omnipresence. This is my desire. I would be eternally grateful for any assistance in this endeavor."

The Father then said, "As you wish, but do not forget that I am in Nature; that also wherever there is life, I am!" and he returned the man to his body, which was in the process of being revived. The man did not remember all that took place, but his life shifted that day. He began a series of experiences that allowed him to remember. He is now walking among humanity, speaking with those who ask, reminding them of the true nature of God. He carries no doctrine or scripture, only an open door to a higher consciousness and energy. He speaks to simple people, the meek and the higher consciousness, and energy flows through him like a river.

The Carpenter & the Law

There was a boy who, at a very young age, showed the promise of genius. He was very sensitive, and he seemed to be aware of everything in his environment. He was often seen gazing at the stars and having conversations with unseen entities. He was keen of intellect, and he often baffled the wisest of men. Some considered him a saint; some were envious and jealous; while others called him possessed-in league with the devil.

As he grew, so did his powers. The wind was at his beck and call. Nature seemed to do whatever he commanded. He knew the innermost thoughts of everyone, and he often counseled them about the benefits of focusing on love and joy. Many found this intimidating. Rather than changing themselves and healing, they tried to deny his credibility. As more and more gathered around the young man, those who held positions in government and religious organizations began to feel insecure. His teachings did not support their superior roles. The love, joy, freedom and equality of his words started a movement that shook the very foundations of society.

He was also endowed with the ability to heal. His wisdom and kind deeds were known throughout the land. Everything he focused his attention on was enhanced. His carpentry was a reflection of his creativity, and the structures he built had specific forms to guide unseen energies. They were built in a fashion unknown to most men. His techniques for healing went beyond any recognized form of treatment. His wisdom went far beyond psychology and physics. He was truly an example of omniscient mind.

In the light of his example, those in authority became acutely aware of their own inadequacies, and they felt threatened. They feared losing their positions, their wealth and the style of living to which they were accustomed. The young carpenter found opposition at every turn. He was ordered to cease preaching, because he was not an ordained minister. He was ordered to refuse any funds to support his vision because he had not registered with the government and acquired the necessary tax number. He was not allowed to build, because the structures he created did not conform to codes. They were not built in a manner the authorities could understand. Though his structures were solid and safe, they were unacceptable.

The carpenter was also ordered to cease his healing practice because he was unlicensed and did not hold a degree in a medical field. Though his counsel was far beyond the wisest of men, he was ordered not to counsel anyone because, again, he was unlicensed and he was not educated by an accredited institution.

The young carpenter heard cries of thousands asking for his counsel and his healing touch, but his hands were tied. He went into the wilderness to contemplate a way out of this dilemma. He spent days and nights praying for a solution. His words were, "Father, beloved Father, I hear their cries. I am driven from within to console and heal. I desire nothing for myself other than the freedom to follow what I am driven to. Show me the way, Father. Let thy will be mine. To this I surrender."

After seven days he returned. He was not the same. He had a glow about him. His confusion was replaced by a direct knowing of purpose and of what he must do. You could see it in his eyes and feel it in his countenance. He called the people to meet him on a hilltop. Thousands gathered, including the authorities who had the necessary papers to arrest him for holding a gathering without a permit. The authorities were ordered to wait and register the number of people he healed and counseled to add to the charges.

As the sun rose, the people moved about, stretching and warming themselves with the morning sun. As the young carpenter took to the top of the hill, the masses moved forward, all getting as close as they could. They began to cheer and chant his name. With his loving gaze upon them, he raised his arms with outstretched palms. As he lowered his hands, the crowd became quiet, awaiting his message.

He spoke. "Beloved brothers and sisters, I am neither higher nor lower than any one of you. I am the example of what you truly are, beyond fear, unworthiness and ignorance. I am an example of the love, joy and power in all of you. There are those who would like to keep you in darkness. They are among you this day. I love them just as I love each and every one of you. I understand the fear and confusion that makes them do what they do. They have bound and tied my heart just as they have bound and tied yours. I have been controlled, manipulated and intimidated, just as you have. They have taken away my freedom to do what I am driven to do, what brings me joy. I can no longer dream, build, counsel or heal, for it is forbidden by their law.

"There is a sacred law that will prevail. It is the law of love. It allows you the freedom to do what is within your heart, what brings you joy. Those who wish to control and enslave are themselves controlled and enslaved. They must follow me just as they must follow you, because their next move is determined by ours. They have given up the freedom to do what truly brings them joy and are themselves enslaved by those they wish to dominate. Their days are numbered.

"I must go now, but I will never leave you. I will come again, but not as you see me now. I will come from within. I will nurture you, guide you, heal you, lift and empower you. My mission will continue. It cannot and will not fail. I shall not rest until all of humanity is awakened to the God within. I go on to the Father, but do not look for me in the ethers. I am within you just as God is within you. I am the pure, unconditional love, joy and freedom within. I am the sacred law."

With those words the heavens trembled. The young carpenter rose into the air above the crowds. He seemed to explode into a brilliant light. Those who resisted him most and those who came to arrest him were knocked flat to the ground. Everyone was healed and freed of their burdens. His last words came from the heavens, "I am within you. I am within your neighbor. Where there is life, I am. Do not judge me no matter what form I take. Love me unconditionally, as I have loved you unconditionally. I am within. I am love."

As the people descended from the hill, they each carried with them a part of the carpenter. They had a new look in their eyes. It was a look of courage and determination. The confusion was gone, and each knew his own unique purpose. All they needed was an example to remind them of the loving, joyous God that resides within them.

The Man with Two Bottles

In a peaceful village lived a simple man who was at peace with himself, yet a part of him yearned for the rich life. He often sat alongside the stream that flowed through his village and contemplated a life of riches and fame. One day, when he came to his favorite spot where he played out his fantasies in his imagination, there sat a stranger with two bottles in his hand. The simple man asked, "What brings you to this neck of the woods?" The stranger said, "I was guided to come to this place and pass these two bottles on to the first one I meet."

The simple man asked what was in the bottles. The stranger told him the first bottle contained oil which, if dabbed on the forehead just above and between the eyes, would bring untold riches and manifest anything you can imagine. The simple man's heart beat faster. His imagination went wild and he had to have the bottle. He asked the stranger how much the bottle would cost him. The stranger told the simple man that though the bottle was free, it would cost him his integrity and his soul-things far more valuable than the contents of the bottle.

The simple man asked the stranger, "If I take the bottle, will someone or something take my integrity and my soul?" The stranger replied, "No, that will be done by your own hand, in your own time, under your own control-or lack of it." The simple man thought about the stranger's statement. He decided if all was under his control and done by his own hand, he could experience all the riches the bottle had to offer without consequence. After all, if it was done at his own hand, he would have total control of the outcome.

He asked the stranger what was in the second bottle. The stranger told him the second bottle would undo and dissolve all that was created by the first bottle and return the simple man to his original state. It contained the essence of forgiveness, wisdom and impeccable integrity. It would dissolve everything except the wisdom gained from the experience.

The simple man confidently snatched the bottles and thanked the stranger. As the stranger left, he turned to the simple man and told him, "In the beginning you will be extremely grateful. When the first bottle is empty you will become very angry. And in the end you will again be grateful. Remember these words. It is never too late."

The simple man did not waste a moment. He dabbed the oil on his forehead and imagined a trunk of gold. Low and behold, a trunk of gold manifested before him. He nearly killed himself dragging it back to the village. He looked at his simple hut and said to himself, "This is no way for a rich man to live." He sat on his trunk and again dabbed the oil on his forehead, imagining a stately palace. The next moment he was sitting on his trunk of gold and underneath it were beautiful marble floors. He was surrounded by a beautiful palace.

Soon his palace, though expansive, felt empty. He decided to have a banquet and invite all of his friends. People came from all over. Aristocrats and others that in the past would not give him the time of day, came to his banquet. Everyone had an opinion about what he should do with his money, how he should live his life and whom he should call his friends. The aristocrats told him he could not hang out with commoners or village rabble. They said his funds could buy him a place in the aristocracy. Still, some of the aristocrats would never allow him into their world because he lacked the proper bloodline.

The simple man's poor friends told him not to get involved with the aristocracy. They suggested his funds would best be used to help the commoners better their positions in life. Some of his former friends were jealous and resented his newfound wealth. They would not have anything to do with him.

His true friends told him that they would be his friends always, rich or poor, and whatever he decided to do was up to him. They did not need his money and held him in high regard despite any position bestowed upon him.

He desired a companion to support him and guide him in his decisions. Once again, out came the bottle. His mind was still leaning towards his former fantasies, and moments later a beautiful woman of lineage and wealth knocked upon his door. She supported him and guided him according to her world. Soon he was a man of position and great wealth, and he governed many.

After a few years passed, the man had his fill of the complicated life of rules, regulations and socially acceptable behavior that went with his position. He began to long for a simpler life. He no longer wanted to make decisions for anyone but himself. The demands of this new way of life and his female companion had taken away his freedom and his joy. There was too much social pressure. No longer could he follow the itinerary set by his wife.

The demands and needs of those he governed became overwhelming. He began to hate his wife, the aristocracy and those he governed because he blamed them for taking away his joy. He wanted back the simple life, that he now fully appreciated. He decided to return to his former life, but when he opened the first bottle, it was empty. His wife entered the room and demanded that he straighten out and stop this madness. She told him people were talking about his behavior of late, making remarks such as, "Once a commoner always a commoner"; "Blood determines aristocracy, not money"; and other slanderous remarks. She also demanded more gold to fund her many endeavors and to buy lavish jewels and dresses to help maintain her status.

The man found his trunk empty. He also found that his so-called friends, in whom he had trusted and invested his money, had done well for themselves, but not so well for him. His debts greatly exceeded his assets, and soon, rumors destroyed his credibility and position in the aristocracy. His wife left shortly thereafter to find another who could finance her whims and offer her a new, more permanent position in the aristocracy.

The once simple man became angry and bitter. He hated his wife and the aristocracy, and he cursed the man who gave him the bottles. In doing so, he remembered the stranger telling him about the time that he would be grateful, followed by a time of anger. The simple man decided he wanted his old friends and his old way of life back. He left the remains of his kingdom, only to find his old way of life and his friends had vanished. They had been driven out by his many business ventures and by those he trusted with his fortune. His old village was now a sprawling city, the center of which was filled with businesses he had financed.

He realized what he had done, and he wept. He begged for forgiveness within himself, forgiveness from his former friends, and forgiveness for his own ignorance and foolishness. He spent the next few days on the outskirts of the city weeping, tormented by his deeds and by a simple life he once loved and could not return to.

When his eyes finally cleared, the sorrow left, and he realized he was in his favorite spot of old alongside the stream. It had been spared his ignorance and unbridled greed. A great joy came upon him, and the words ran through his mind, "It is never too late." He remembered the second bottle. He remembered it would dissolve all that which was created by the first bottle.

He also remembered it contained the essence of forgiveness, wisdom and impeccable integrity. He ran back to the remains of his palace, which had been raped and stripped of anything of value by his creditors who were once his friends. He remembered that he hid the second bottle because he feared it would someday be the demise of his kingdom. But, he could not remember where. Yet, he knew if he searched within himself, he would remember where the bottle, along with its essence, was hidden.

After days of searching, contemplating and remembering, it came to him. He hid the bottle in a tree trunk at the entrance to his favorite spot at the head of the stream. He could not return to the spot for fear of remembering, so he hid it at the entrance. He returned to the entrance and did not hesitate to dab the oil from the second bottle on his forehead, imagining how things once were. As he came out of his dream, everything had returned. The village was the same, and his friends were all there living their simple, joyous life.

The return dissolved all guilt, for it was as if nothing had ever happened. This allowed the man to even forgive himself. All that remained was the wisdom gained from the experience. This wisdom gave him the impeccable integrity and steadfastness not to act ignorantly or foolishly, or to be swayed by the will of others. The once simple man was again a simple man, yet his old desires and fantasies were fulfilled. The yearning was over. He was once again extremely grateful to the stranger-most of all for the second bottle, the second chance and the wisdom gained from the experience. The greatest gift of all were the words, "It is never too late."

Which bottle are you using?

The Mud People

In a far-off galaxy, there was a boy named Ranoah. He was one of many who lived in a society of honorable people with great integrity. They were highly advanced morally and technologically. Their police force consisted of a brotherhood that kept the peace throughout the galaxy. They were known as elite warriors of the universe, and it was every boy's dream to become one. Ranoah was no different, and he often fantasized about becoming a warrior in the force.

The years went by, and Ranoah was approaching manhood. His family had a long history of men in the Brotherhood. His uncle was an admiral. On Ranoah's nineteenth birthday, his uncle knocked on his door, package in hand. Ranoah quickly opened the package and found his dream had come true. The package held a uniform and all the necessary documentation to enter the Brotherhood.

Ranoah's mother had hoped he would break tradition and choose a different profession, but Ranoah's heart was set. He had heard too many stories filled with adventure. A week later Ranoah was in the compound of the Brotherhood, studying their codes and disciplines.

The training was arduous, physically and mentally.

Four years passed, and it was time for graduation. Ranoah graduated with top honors, and his family and friends were proud. He was knighted into the Brotherhood and was walking on air. He was now a man. He believed he would never truly be a man until he became a warrior in the Brotherhood.

His first assignment was under the command of Captain Zacal, a seasoned and honorable man, well decorated for his achievements and bravery in the Brotherhood. Zacal met Ranoah with a smile and a look of approval. He told Ranoah that he was very impressed with his files and that he had been watching him as he developed. Ranoah replied with admiration and gratefulness.

They walked down a long corridor and entered the landing bay. There was a fleet of polished shuttles. Zacal looked at his papers and walked over to the shuttle that corresponded with the numbers on the page. He walked around it, inspecting all sides. He pushed a button on the side to break the airlock and the door lifted, exposing an instrument panel at the front of the craft. The craft itself was box-like with skids underneath. Long cylinders were attached to the skids. These were part of the propulsion system.

Zacal entered the shuttle and beckoned Ranoah to follow. He handed Ranoah a belt with an attached laser and a few other devices used by the Brotherhood for defense. Ranoah received the highest marks in defense. When Zacal asked him if he knew how to use them, he just smiled and nodded. They closed the door and within moments after lifting off, they were in deep space.

Zacal explained the mission to Ranoah. It was a routine mission to Tazarus. Tazarus was a red planet rich in crystals and rare minerals. They were necessary to build and propel their craft, as well as meet the energy needs of their people. A few moments later they were hovering over an outpost and the shuttle landed softly on the dusty road.

Ranoah assisted the merchant in loading and securing the cargo while Zacal stood at the front of the shuttle. Ranoah heard a grumbling sound that resembled a chant. It grew louder, and when he emerged from the shuttle he saw a large crowd of what seemed to be disenchanted people surrounding the shuttle.

Zacal told Ranoah to button things up, that it was time to leave. Ranoah slammed the rear door and moved towards the front of the shuttle. As he moved around the shuttle he saw three of the people coming up behind Zacal. Zacal was grabbing for his laser and didn't see them. Ranoah dove behind Zacal and took out all three. He pulled his laser and stunned them before Zacal even knew what happened. Zacal looked at Ranoah with a sigh of relief and thanked him. "I'm getting too old for this," he said.

The rest of the people backed up for a moment, gathered their courage and again began to move closer. Their chants became louder as they worked up their courage. They seemed to be lethargic, and their legs were covered with mud. Zacal motioned Ranoah to get into the shuttle, and in a moment they were both preparing for lift-off.

The Mud People charged the shuttle, beating it with sticks and rocks. As it lifted up above the dusty road a few were still clinging to the skids. Zacal reached for the panel and maneuvered the shuttle over a nearby lake. He flicked a switch that electrified the skids and the Mud People screamed as they fell into the water. "They never learn," Zacal said with a grin. Ranoah asked Zacal who the Mud People were and why were they attacking them.

Zacal explained to Ranoah the history of the Mud People. They were controlled and enslaved by their priests. One of their priests wore mud on his legs to prevent himself from being bitten by an insect indigenous to the area.

The insects would hop on a person's leg and bite. It was very painful. These insects could only jump just above the ankle, so the priest's method of prevention proved very effective. The people thought applying mud was a ritual to make the priests more holy, so they adopted the practice. The people have all kinds of rituals to appease their God that are really quite humorous.

Ranoah understood why they wore the mud, but he still didn't understand why they hated the Brotherhood. Zacal explained why on the way to their next stop. He told Ranoah that the priests lost control of any person who spent any length of time with a member of the Brotherhood. In the company of a Brother, a Mud person would eventually become independent. He would even smile and become less lethargic because he gained hope and found something to live for. The priests introduced new codes into their doctrines as a last ditch effort to keep control. The priests promise that if a person dies in an attack against the Brotherhood, he will gain entry into what they call heaven.

"The Mud people know we could obliterate them in a moment, but they also know it is against our code to be the aggressor. We can only provide protection to those who ask. It is also our code to never back down or appear to be weak. We have a reputation to keep. If we appear to be weak, it will only put those whom we protect in danger."

Rajas 9 was now on the screen, and in moments the shuttle was again settling down on another dusty road. It was similar to Tazarus and was inhabited by the same people. Ranoah wasted no time and went about his duties loading and securing the cargo. Zacal went to the front of the shuttle and told Ranoah there was nothing to worry about, that it would take the Mud people a while to work up the nerve to do anything. Ranoah closed the door to the back of the shuttle and moved around to the front to assist Zacal.

The Mud People gathered much more rapidly than before and were already moving towards Zacal and the shuttle. They seemed to be prepared this time, and they acted as if they remembered Zacal. Zacal pulled his laser, turned it to stun and said, "Remember this boys?" There were hundreds of them and they kept advancing and climbing over the ones Zacal stunned. The lasers soon drained, and it turned into hand-to-hand combat. Minutes seemed like hours, and though both Zacal and Ranoah were highly trained in self-defense, they soon grew weary. Ranoah had taken on the major portion of the battle due to his youth and stamina. He fought with all his heart to save Zacal, but it wasn't enough.

The last thing Ranoah remembered was a loud bell and a crack over the head. Ranoah's next vision was that of a beautiful woman standing over him. This vision of heaven was shattered when he heard Zacal's voice asking him if he was still with them. Ranoah was confused. He didn't understand how he survived or how he ended up in this room.

Zacal explained to him about the temple bells. "There are a few Mud People in the temple loyal to the Brotherhood. They saw we needed help, so they rang the bells. The Mud People, being of strict discipline, dropped everything and ran to the temple. Some people call it running, it looks more like a fast shuffle."

Ranoah told Zacal his head was still spinning and he needed some time to recuperate. Zacal said he would return to the outpost in three days. He told Ranoah he was safe and in another compound on Rajas 9 under the protection of the Brotherhood.

Ranoah spent the next three days contemplating the rigid codes and disciplines of the Mud People, as well as the rigid codes and disciplines of the Brotherhood. He thought about violence and the reasoning behind it. He also knew there must be a better way to obtain what they needed without violence. He had experienced enough violence and saw no honor in it. He remembered the faces of the Mud People who kept coming and coming. He welcomed the board that hit him on the head. He had hurt so many of them he began to feel sorry for them. The Brotherhood, the crystals and minerals, even his own life, had lost any meaning towards the end of the battle.

The days passed quickly and on the night of the third day, Zacal was standing at the foot of his bed. Ranoah asked Zacal why the Brotherhood could not land in an unmarked shuttle without their uniforms to pick up their cargo. Other civilizations have no trouble. Zacal told him it was against their code, and to sneak out like a rat would be degrading. Ranoah again asked if it was worth the risk to our people as well as the harm it brings to the Mud People. "If we can avoid violence at any cost, it would be worth it. After all, are we not known as the keepers of the peace?"

Zacal reminded Ranoah of the codes and disciplines of the Brotherhood. He told him, "We are the law, and the law must be upheld at any cost." Ranoah again asked Zacal if he would reason that the tradition of the Brotherhood is what is creating the violence and we were created to be keepers of the peace.

Zacal was getting a bit angry and was looking desperately for an excuse to validate holding on to the old traditions, especially when he had fought all his life to uphold them. He finally replied in a half-hearted voice, "They are only barbarians, and they need to be taught a lesson." Ranoah replied, "We too were once barbarians who share a history very similar to the Mud People. I am very grateful some advanced race didn't come down to teach us a lesson. After all, we probably wouldn't be here today if they had." Zacal had a look of sadness and betrayal in his eyes. He gathered up Ranoah's uniform and told him he had great hopes for Ranoah. He also told him he could not serve the Brotherhood if his heart was not in it. With a look of disgust he left the room.

The nurse came in and comforted Ranoah. She told him he had made the right decision. She wished there were more men like him with enough courage to follow their heart. She also said she had patched up enough young men.

Ranoah acquired a robe worn by the common people of Rajas 9. He grew to love them and allowed them to evolve at their own pace. He chose to help those who asked and is still with them today. He is known as the Father of Rajas 9. They no longer wear mud, and they have been at peace for years. Their planet flourishes. Rajas 9 is now known as an Eden in a galaxy far away.

The Consortium

In a great hall, far away in a distant galaxy, there was a gathering of peoples. It was known as the consortium, which consisted of a myriad of ambassadors from other planes, other dimensions and other universes. The topic of the day was Earth. There was a heated debate as to whether to risk allowing the co-creating experiment of free will and powerful emotions to continue or to wipe the slate clean and start over with new seed.

To many this action-reaction world, known as the plane of demonstration, where consciousness creates reality, was a mistake that if not erased would leak out into the rest of the universe. They found the actions of the people of Earth disgusting and intolerable. They cited case after case of warlike behavior, unbridled greed and decadence. They saw a civilization bent upon not only destroying itself, but also the very platform for life upon which they resided. They were also very concerned with the rapid growth and misuse of technology that was outpacing the evolution of spirituality and the acceptance of basic universal principles.

Humanity, with its nuclear experimentation, was fragmenting the Earth's crust and disrupting the very fabric of space, creating a ripple effect felt throughout the universe. They believed the experiment known as Earth was a grand failure and must be terminated before it did any more damage, or spread out into the rest of the universe. Unfortunately they had a very good case backed by enormous evidence.

There was another group, many of which had ascended from Earth as masters, saints and avatars along with other advanced beings, who pleaded on the behalf of humanity and the Earth. There were advanced beings who came from other planes, dimensions and galaxies, and they gave compassionate pleas citing their own ancient history where they, too, were once warlike, lusting for power and money at the expense of their people and their planet. They also had their decadent factions. They came very close to completely annihilating themselves, yet they crossed that threshold, leaving it far behind in their evolution. Love is now the manifesting force behind all creation, and their technology is a reflection of their spirituality.

The masters who ascended from the Earth also pleaded on behalf of those who have dedicated their lives in service to God, humanity and the Earth, many of who were also on the threshold of ascension. "Their efforts must not be in vain, nor go unrewarded. We cannot abandon them. What they need is more time and some divine intervention on all our parts, along with a little more patience honoring their evolutionary process." The debate continued for days in time as we know it, and, as each side spoke, holograms appeared high in the center of the great hall providing visual historical evidence to defend their positions. After the final closing statements, there was a long silence followed by an adjournment.

The meeting reconvened as the head of the consortium entered the hall and took his position along with the twelve other panel members. As the murmuring of the crowd diminished, the head of the consortium rose and began to speak. He was very tall and majestic with long golden hair and a beard to match, which flowed into his golden white robes. His body was not physical as we know it. It consisted of magnetized light for the convenience of those who needed a focal point, yet, in truth, he was pure consciousness that expanded into infinity.

He began by informing the consortium that they had reached a decision concerning the destiny of Earth and all its inhabitants. He also informed them that all that has transpired has been taken into account, and he expressed great admiration for all who have spoken. "The points have well been made, and we are very concerned about Earth's destiny. We have watched other civilizations transcend their baser nature and evolve into the grandeur of what now sits among us. We have watched others annihilate themselves, turning their planets into desolate wastelands, some of which exploded and are now meteors and asteroids. They could not overcome their unbridled greed and lust for power. They failed to realize the ultimate power of the universe, the eternal everlasting power of love, the manifesting force behind all creation. Love always empowers, never overpowers, and always acts in the highest and best good of all life for where there is life, there is God.

"Many of these souls are residing upon the Earth as we speak. They have been given a second chance to utilize the wisdom gained from the past and to once again choose. The Earth is at a turning point where all must choose. The awakening and healing of humanity and the Earth is no longer optional. A great light shall come upon the Earth. It will be known as the quickening.

"Those who choose love to be the manifesting force behind all creation will be exalted. Those who choose to continue in their againstness, unbridled greed and lust for power at the expense of humanity will suffer the reactions to their actions straight away. All lower vibrational attitudes and emotions and their physical counterparts will be lifted, healed, and in some cases, the temples will fall. The divine right to free will and self-determination shall still be honored. Each individual will be at his own hand held accountable for his own choices. This special dispensation of energy will be a blessing to some and an enemy to others who resist the light and love of their very God-selves. Nature will play her part in delivering the reactions, cleansing all that harms her. These will be perilous times for some, exciting times for others. Those who can align themselves and flow with these changes shall see a new Earth appear, a new civilization emerge, and the heavens open, revealing kingdoms and civilizations beyond their wildest dreams. It shall be known as the age of God. It is destiny, and no man can stop it. So shall it be."

The Return

"My son, it is good to see you again. I have been away nigh a long time now."

"Who are you?"

"I am the all that is the all. I am life in all forms. I am within you, I am you-the you long since forgotten."

"Why are you here?"

"I am everywhere. Where there is life, I am."

"What do you wish of me?"

"I wish to see my garden-Eden, as you know it. What have you done with it?"

"Eden was a long time ago. This is the twentieth century."

"What does time have to do with something created to be eternal?"

"Over time we have not done a very good job of holding it together. It seems to have slipped through our fingers a little at a time.

"Show me what you have done with this heaven called Earth, which I have left in your care."

"Well, we have built large cities with restaurants, hotels and skyscrapers."

"That is very nice, but what has happened to the animals that were so abundant, the rivers, the forests that once were there? What have you done with the life that I am?"

"The trees went to lumber to build the cities. The water from the rivers had to be controlled, so it has been diverted through concrete ditches and sewers until it finally ends up in the ocean."

"I created the trees to hold the water, to shade the land and to regulate the rate at which the snow melts. These were the controls that monitored the water. They were created for the shelter of man as well as animals, which are one and the same. I am not averse to partaking of the trees responsibly or selectively, but to take a place teeming with life-that which I am and lay it to waste, that, dear one, is a sin against life. Where are the fish, the birds and the bear?"

"Well, the fish cannot live in the ditches because the concrete does not allow the mosses, grasses and foliage needed to sustain them. Also, the water is polluted in many ways."

"How did this come about?"

"We decided to gain more free time, by creating machines and processing plants to provide for our needs. These plants give off waste products which run through the ditches into the rivers and eventually out to the sea."

"Has this given you more free time? Are you not now slaves to these machines and the jobs they create?"

"Well, yes, in a way, but look how abundant we are."

"Did you know that one kernel of corn will grow thousands of kernels, which again will grow millions of kernels? If you tended your garden for four months out of the year, you could take the other eight off. When I left this plane, everything was simple, abundant and balanced. You have told me about the fish. Now where are the birds?"

"The birds could not sustain themselves because we leveled the ground and paved it for cars to drive and people to walk. This enables us to move from one place to another more quickly."

"Do the machines that travel these roads also own you?"

"They do."

"If you had not become so complicated and confused, you would have evolved to a state where transportation would not be necessary. All you would have to do is to think of where you wanted to go and you would be there. I will not ask where the bear has gone, for I have heard enough. I have come at this time because so many have called. There are those who remember the garden and see what is being done to life. They know of the reaction about to come, due to the actions of man. Those who have acted irresponsibly will be exposed. That which they laid to waste will come back to haunt them. When I created Eden and gave man dominion, it was as a caretaker.

"Look around you and see what you have done to the very platform that sustains you. The streams and lakes are muddied and poisoned. The sky is gray and has a stench. Endless miles of forest have been laid to waste, as well as the animals that inhabited them. Plains and valleys are now asphalt and concrete. The water that was meant to sustain life, moisten and lubricate the plates on which you sit, is all being diverted to poison the oceans. The oceans are now rising. The planet is heating up, as well as being poisoned above and below. All in the name of progress. Progress, without respect for life, will end in the collapse of civilization as you know it. This is not the first civilization that has done itself in.

"I will leave you to your progress, so that where you are progressing will teach you something. If success is more important than life, so be it. I have given man a divine right, free will and dominion over this world.

"I shall not go back on my word. Therefore, it is up to man to clean up his own mess and begin manifesting responsibly to the glory of God, which is life."

Skunk & the High Places

Once upon a time there was Skunk. Skunk was very lonely, sarcastic in nature, and he went about his daily business insensitive to others. Wherever he went, he left a trail of bad odors and bad feelings. He seldom had anything nice to say, and he cared nothing for his environment or the needs of others. All he cared for were his own self-interests. He was a sad and lonely skunk indeed.

Mrs. Skunk, his wife, was of the same nature. She would often find new, unspoiled land, rich and abundant with food. Together they would move in, displacing all the other creatures until the land became a reflection of their attitudes and emotions. It was soon laid barren. With a stench, the Skunks, along with their unbridled greed, selfishness and inconsiderate natures, were off to a new adventure. The Skunks were known throughout the forest by their attitudes, emotions and deeds. They were disliked, to say the least.

The Skunks had an innate desire to be loved. Deep within their hearts they wanted to be accepted, appreciated and admired by the community. They talked it over one day and thought if only they were held high in the hearts and minds of the rest of the forest dwellers, they would be happy. They thought of the bear, the eagle and the elk who were held in high esteem. So, the very next day, Mrs. Skunk sent Skunk to find them a home high in the mountains. They believed that if they moved to a high place and made it their home, the other forest dwellers would look up to them.

On his way, Skunk first encountered Bear, who was going about his business feeding on grubs and termites in a rotten log. Skunk, in line with his selfish and inconsiderate nature, decided to move in and take what the bear had found, using his foul odor and a spray in the face if necessary. Bear told Skunk, with a growl, that he was trespassing and had no right to foul his dinner. Skunk told Bear that he took whatever he needed, whenever he wanted, and did not honor anyone's borders.

Bear took his stand and Skunk took his, backing up to the bear and releasing his foul odor. Bear, being of stout heart and courage, braved the odor, knowing he would have to live with it for a long while. The suffering inflicted by Skunk was worth enduring because Bear's respect for justice and his fearless reputation were worth defending at any cost.

Though thoroughly sprayed, Bear managed a powerful swat that sent Skunk flying and tumbling down the mountain. Skunk was battered and bruised, and he left with a clawed and tender rear as a reminder of the reaction to his actions. But Skunk, still desperate to live on high, tried an alternate route to the high places. On his new route he met Elk. Elk was eating huckleberries that were so ripe they were splitting at the seams. Elk's face was a reflection of a noble and powerful creature, with a childlike delight at consuming the berries.

Skunk, again true to his nature, decided to move in and take the berries for himself. His thoughts were of Mrs. Skunk and how proud she would be if he brought home all the berries. Elk saw Skunk backing up the hill and Elk knew just what to do. He had dealt with skunks before. Elk moved to the side of the trail and waited for Skunk to pass. As Skunk passed Elk, he was looking behind him, expecting Elk to leave or attack him, upon which he would deliver his spray directly into the face of Elk. Elk, being a very clever animal, allowed Skunk to pass and jumped onto the trail. Before Skunk could redirect his spray, Elk scooped him up in his antlers and flung him through the air, eventually to go crashing down the mountain.

Skunk had another chance to reevaluate his actions as well as his attitude, for he had again met with a painful and violent reaction to his actions. Skunk, battered and torn, returned home with stories of the high places where mountain animals do not act the way the lowland animals act. He told Mrs. Skunk, "Although my spray is foul and agonizing, it is always met with courage, self-authority and cleverness."

Mrs. Skunk was determined to live in the high places. She had been dreaming of being held in high regard, and now it was of the utmost importance. She sent Skunk out again, the very next day, to find a high place in which they could live.

Skunk was clever in his own way, but his cleverness was no match for the high thinkers on the mountain. Skunk decided that, if he took the rocky and barren trail, he would not be met with any resistance, and he would make it to the highest peaks unchallenged. His journey was long and treacherous, with many rockslides and cliffs, but eventually he reached a high plateau. He was starving. There had been little to eat on his journey. As he rested, he smelled fish. He wondered how a fish had gotten to this barren, rocky plateau. He followed the scent to a weathered and twisted tree upon which sat Eagle.

Eagle was a grand spectacle of noble power and wisdom. Skunk, reflecting on his past lessons and the awesome majestic power of Eagle, decided his standard approach would not bear fruit. Eagle, seeing all and knowing all, asked Skunk if he had learned anything from his encounters with Bear and Elk. Skunk replied that he had, and that he realized he was out of his class and element.

Eagle told Skunk he was born of the same Father God as himself, Bear and Elk and that there were no classes or hierarchies. There is only God. Again Eagle asked Skunk what he had learned. Skunk replied, "If I am born of the same Father, why do the others treat me with such offense?"

Eagle answered, "I am God expressing as an eagle. Bear is God expressing as a bear. Elk is God expressing as an elk. And, you are God expressing as a skunk. You do not know that you are God. All you know is skunk. If you knew you also were God, you would see the brotherhood-the family-and you would treat the rest of creation as brothers and family. You are as important as the eagle, the bear, and the elk, yet you are neither more important nor less important. You are equal. You have neither honored this equality nor respected the rights of others, because you do not honor the God within yourself that loves and honors the whole of life evenly, respectfully and with great compassion.

"You gazed upon my fish and considered fouling this sacred place for a mere fish. You have learned from Bear and Elk to honor the rights of others and not to foul sacred places with your spray. Their courage, self-authority and cleverness will not allow you to do so."

Skunk was humbled by the wisdom of Eagle. He asked Eagle to have mercy on him. Skunk apologized for his thoughts and asked Eagle if he would also deliver his apology to Bear and Elk for his selfish trespasses. Eagle flew straight away, dropping his fish at the feet of Skunk with a message in his passing, "There is enough for everyone, and you need not take from or trespass on anyone."

The fish was enormous. It fed Skunk for three days. Skunk bathed himself in mountain streams, rolled in the flowers, basked in the sun and, for once in his life, found joy. There was no one to judge him or condemn him, and now he realized that he was God expressing as a skunk.

He also realized that a skunk is divine and can behave divinely-unconditionally loving, allowing and honoring the rest of creation evenly, knowing they were born of the same Father and were one family. Skunk began his trek down the mountain. He did not follow the rocky and treacherous path, for now he accepted himself, loved himself, and knew if he honored the God within others and did not trespass, he would be accepted and honored by those in high places.

Skunk came upon Bear, who was busy with another gourmet meal of grubs. Skunk bowed and apologized for his offensive behavior. Bear, with a wise and powerful smile, bowed to Skunk and offered what was left of his feast.

Further down the path, skunk came upon Elk. Elk told Skunk he had spoken to Eagle and there was no need to apologize. Elk also invited Skunk to join him while he dined on the huckleberries. Skunk agreed, and after a few berries he continued on his journey down the mountain.

On his return home, Skunk was met by Mrs. Skunk. She saw the change and was threatened by it. She asked Skunk if he had staked out and claimed their new territory in high places. Skunk told Mrs. Skunk there was no need to stake out and claim territory. There was plenty for all. This was a blow to Mrs. Skunk's security, yet she listened as Skunk told her about his encounter with Bear, Elk and the wisdom of Eagle. He told her about the respect he had earned through humility and honoring and respecting the rights of others. He told her he was God expressing as a skunk. He told her when she understood this and loved and accepted herself, honoring the God in all creation without trespassing, others would love and accept her.

The Skunks never moved, but they are living in a very high place. They gained the love and respect of the forest dwellers by teaching them that they were all unique expressions of God, and to love and accept themselves and others, knowing the God in all life. Their foul odor left, for they no longer used or needed it. They lived a long and prosperous life, admired and held in highest regard in the hearts and minds of the forest dwellers.

Land of Sevals

Rosserpo[2] was the king of the land of Sevals. His kingdom was one of oppression. The people were owned and subject to his whims. All those who rebelled were eliminated, except the few who were clever enough to evade the King's henchmen by escaping to faraway lands. The king hired assassins to seek out and destroy these brave souls, to let the people know that there was no place to hide.

There was a council known as the "Council of Sredraoh." They advised the king and financed his endeavors. They were the fuel behind

---

2. Note: The names of the individuals and organizations have meaning if you read them backwards.

every war. They preyed upon the ambition of the king, lavishly praising him for all of his victories. They explained to the king that if he taxed the people sufficiently, he would have the funds necessary to rule the world. The council would, of course, provide the weapons and guidance necessary to complete the task.

The Seesirahp was the religious order in the land of Sevals. It, too, was owned and controlled by the Council of Sredraoh. The king, the Council and the Seesirahp held a meeting to plan the demise of the adjoining country, Evol, and the lords that governed Evol. The Lords of Evol were holy men. They assisted and guided the people of Evol in the peaceful and abundant manner in which they existed. They were hated by the Sredraoh and the Seesirahp, because they were the truth and the light.

The Lords of Evol governed not through fear or manipulation, but by love and freedom. They were chosen for their humbleness, clarity and desire for the good of all. They were known by the light that surrounded their heads and hands. They could heal with a touch. They loved and cherished an all-merciful, loving God that was the life force within all things. They were lovers of the land. Everything they created was beautiful and in harmony with nature. They truly lived in paradise. The light that surrounded their heads allowed them unlimited knowledge.

Although the king of Sevals took every precaution to hold his meeting in secret, the Lords knew all that transpired. They watched as the priests of the Seesirahp spoke of the evils of Evol. The people of Sevals were told that God would punish them if Evol was allowed to continue. Various doctrines were quoted concerning the evils of abundance, and the people of Sevals were told that dying in a holy war against Evol would insure their passage to heaven.

The people of Sevals were stirring in religious fervor. The captain of the army began spreading rumors about the people of Evol. He told his warriors that, at that very moment, the people of Evol were planning their march on Sevals. When the people of Sevals were in a sufficient uproar, the king addressed them. He told them, "We must strike first. We must increase our taxes to pay the loans necessary to outfit our armies. I had the foresight to acquire the armies and weapons necessary to save Sevals." He spoke of the necessity of attacking first, before the Evols could organize. He said it was the will of God that Sevals be victorious. His last statement was, "This evil must be annihilated."

After giving his speech, the king was so caught up in the momentum that he began to believe he was doing God's will and that Evol was truly wicked. He could not reflect back and realize that this evil was a fictitious creation. The priests of Sevals were also hypnotized by the fervor of the crowds. The Council of Sredraoh, being very crafty and intelligent, knew the truth, but continued to fuel the emotions of the king and the priests. They had much to gain. The money they made depended on the success of the war.

When the momentum towards war was sufficient and could not be stopped, the Council of Sredraoh went to Evol. They told the people of Evol that an invasion was forthcoming, and that they had to buy weapons to defend themselves against the evil of Sevals. The Council of Sredraoh met with the Lords of Evol and said they would fund their armies, but Evol had no armies. The Council told the Lords that they had the weapons necessary to defend Evol, but the people of Evol did not believe in defense.

Try as they might, the Sredraoh could not arouse fear or anger in the people of Evol. Wherever they went were joy, peace and a brotherly welcome. This so enraged the Council of Sredraoh that they returned to Sevals with a vengeance. They told the people of Sevals that they tried to persuade the Lords of Evol not to war against Sevals, but that the Evols were bent on annihilating every man, woman and child of Sevals.

The Council was enraged at the people of Evol for not buying their weapons. This would be their revenge. The armies of Sevals gathered and began their march against Evol. They were filled with rage and could hardly keep themselves organized. They could not wait to slay their enemy.

There was a large ravine between Evol and Sevals, sided with towering mountains. The ravine opened to the land of Evol and there the Lords of Evol stood. As the armies of Sevals approached, the leader of Evol began to pray, "Father, beloved Father, that which is within all things, that which is in the wind, the rock and the water, protect us now, as we have loved and protected thee. Give these souls what they desire. Allow us to continue in peace."

There was a stillness. The armies of Sevals were baffled. There were no armies facing them, just a few men gathered on a knoll. They seemed to be smiling, with arms outstretched, their palms facing the Sevals. Many Sevals were lifted and healed of their hatred, but most were hard within their hearts. The king of Sevals bellowed, "It's a spell. They are only trying to delay, so their armies can gather. Death to Evol!"

The charge began. The winds began to howl, many were blown from their horses. The dust was so thick that they could not see and began fighting among themselves. Rocks came crashing down from the cliffs and when the dust settled, neither man nor beast was standing.

The people of Evol came to aid the survivors, and they healed them. They sent them back to Sevals as ambassadors of truth. The Council of Sredraoh and the Seesirahp were dispelled from Sevals. The people of Sevals and Evol joined in an alliance of peace, brotherhood and prosperity.

Sredraoh's Return

There was a sleepy, tranquil village at the foot of majestic purple mountains. Its inhabitants were tillers of the soil. They loved their life. A Council of Elders guided the village and solved any disputes, of which there were few.

The Sredraoh, fleeing from Sevals, were welcomed in this village. Many Seesirahp came to the village, but the Sredraoh had already convinced the villagers that the Seesirahp were responsible for the conflict between Sevals and Evol. The Sredraoh told the village Council that they had great wealth and technology to share with the villagers.

The Seesirahp came to the Sredraoh for help because they were penniless and without food or shelter. The Sredraoh told the Seesirahp that they could not stay by order of the village Council. Though they felt sorry for the Seesirahp in their plight, there was nothing they could do. The Council also forbade anyone in the village to assist the Seesirahp, because they were an evil influence. This, of course, was inspired by the Sredraohs. It was necessary to justify hoarding their wealth.

The Sredraoh's first introduction to the village was a monetary system. Up to this point, the people of the village bartered and worked together. They had existed abundantly for thousands of years under this system. The new monetary system made it necessary to place a value on everything. This created status within the village and separated the people. The Council was inundated with disputes as to the value of one job or another.

Many of the necessary jobs, done out of service, did not have the monetary reward to go along with them-thus they were left undone. The jobs that were rewarded the highest were sought out by many. Competition was introduced and, again, the Council was inundated with disputes over who would get the more rewarding jobs.

The Sredraoh knew the Council would buckle under the confusion.

They were not equipped to handle the stress. The Sredraoh offered to handle the situation, and the Council of Elders gladly gave control to the Sredraoh.

The Sredraoh told the Council that civilizations had already established the value of each job. Governments also chose who was best qualified to do each job and rewarded the job to the ones who met these standards. The Sredraoh then began to reward jobs to those who would serve the Sredraoh. Oaths were taken to serve and obey. It was also made known that the value of befriending a Sredraoh was the receipt of gifts and services over and above the call of duty.

Things became more and more complex, and soon, the Council of Elders allowed the Sredraoh to make all the decisions. The Sredraoh gave the Council salaries and positions. They became fat and lazy. All the decisions were made by the Sredraoh. The Council became powerless and idle. Most did not recognize the evil behind the gifts of the Sredraoh, but there were a few within the Council who saw what was happening. They demanded back their power. The Sredraoh, knowing this would come about, had already started rumors concerning the Council.

When the village was gathered by the Council, a spokesman for the Sredraoh charged that the Council with being fat and lazy leeches. He also told the people the Council was being supported by large salaries. The Sredraoh said that they were the true friends of the village, for they were the true servants. The people, in fear of losing their jobs and their status, rebelled, and the Council was cast from the village. The Sredraoh now were in full control, and they began to draw the plans for their empire.

They stoked the ambitions of many with their promises of riches and status within the empire. The forests gave way to their axes, and buildings were erected at a very rapid rate. The open land that was once tilled for crops was now covered with structures, and the farmers expanded outward into the newly opened ground. Where great forests once stood, the cattle now grazed and the ground was being tilled for new crops. The sleepy little village was now a bustling city, ever-expanding like a cancer on the land. Peace and serenity were displaced by ambition and confusion. Love and brotherhood were replaced by greed and competition. Trust was replaced by enforcement agencies.

The Council of Elders was no longer a threat, and they were allowed back into the village, which now was a great city. The Council, seeing the joylessness, sadness and neurosis of this new way of life, tried to remind the people of how things once were. They told them of the peace, the forests and the plentiful fish and game.

They also reminded them that there would be consequences of their actions against nature and their brothers. The people were too busy to listen. To change would mean giving up some of their wealth and status. There was no security in returning to the old ways. Their new way of life was now all they knew, and there was great fear of the unknown. The Council's words fell upon deaf ears. They returned to what was left of the forest and their simplistic way of life.

A dark cloud came across the horizon, and the winds blew like the people had never seen. The forest that once surrounded and protected them was no longer there. Their structures were leveled and tossed like toys. Torrential rains came. The brush and trees necessary to hold the land together were no longer present. Mud slides and flash floods buried and washed away what shelter was left. There were no more stores for food and clothing. All machinery was gone, as well as the roads leading to the village. The old ways had all been forgotten. The game and fish that once fed man no longer existed. The ones that died that day were the lucky ones.

Only a few made it to the forest, which was fortunate, because what was left of the forest could sustain only a few. Those few soon found that the only true peace and security was in aligning with nature and living a simple life. This allowed them once again to experience the joy that lifted them back into the arms of the Father. God, in its purest form, is nature.

The Innkeeper

In a time long since forgotten, there was an innkeeper. He was a pudgy, ambitious little fellow. He was driven by his desire to gather rupees, and he saw himself as a wise trader. To him, it was a game. It was not a matter of honesty, integrity or the good of all concerned. All that mattered was that in the end he was one up. He was very shrewd, and he knew how to create the desire for a thing of fancy and frill. The merchandise he traded was of no practical use. Its only value was what he would instill in the minds of his customers. They soon clung dearly to these trinkets, giving all that they owned to the trader.

Later, it would dawn on the customer that he had been deceived. He had given away all that was of true value. Most became angry, but they were too embarrassed to return to the innkeeper.

A wise old magician came upon the inn. He was tired and thirsty. His only possession was a beautiful book with gold trim. The cover was purple with raised gold letters. It read: *The Secret Of Life*. The innkeeper spotted the book and began his crafty manipulations to acquire it. The magician was very weak with hunger, so the bargain was made. The magician told the man that if he was not pure in heart, the book would bring him harm. It must be used responsibly, for the good of all.

The innkeeper did not hear the magician, for he was already buried in the pages of the book. Because of his nature, his only desire was to find that which would add to his petty little kingdom. The first chapter in the book was "The Creation of Life." This thrilled the man. In this chapter was the formula and the sacred words to create life.

He became obsessed with the power and wisdom in the book. He sold all of his goods to gather the materials needed. True to his nature, he contemplated creating an army of people to govern and do his bidding. He measured and mixed the materials as directed by the book. He then spoke the sacred words and breathed the life into his servants.

What the innkeeper did not realize was that the life he breathed into his creations was the pattern of self. He soon found he could not trust even one of them. They had taken on his attitudes, ideals and emotions.

They reflected the same lack of integrity, dishonesty and desires as their creator. He had to bargain with them for everything. After contemplating his dilemma, he decided to return to the book for a solution. He returned to his room where it all began, only to find one of his creations mixing the elements, book in hand. He snatched the book out of his hands, only to find the chapter on demons, dragons and the underworld. He saw the magic words to bring forth hideous creatures that would do the bidding of their creator.

He turned to his "son" (that which he had created) and asked why he was bringing forth this demon. The son told him he was tired of taking orders and that he wanted to be in control. With the demon, he could control everyone through fear. It was "like father, like son," except that the son had tenfold the iniquities of the father.

The innkeeper became so enraged that he opened the book and spoke the sacred words that withdrew the life force. All of his creations became limp and fell to the ground. He contemplated this experience and remembered the words of the magician, "Only the pure in heart can use this book."

A bit more enlightened, the innkeeper contemplated the past. He still desired to reign over and control a large number of people. This was his need to establish his self-worth. He realized that the breath of life had to come from another source, for he was filled with iniquities. He had a boy in his employ that was the perfect servant. The boy always did as he was told, never questioning. He mixed the elements and called the servant. The servant spoke the words as instructed, thus manifesting the bodies, and breathed in the life known as self.

Soon the innkeeper had an army of servants. The servants had no minds of their own and only wished to serve. They knocked upon his door incessantly, asking what they could do. The innkeeper realized he had become a slave to his servants and had no time of his own. After being totally overwhelmed by his servants, he retired to his room. Again, he spoke the sacred words and withdrew the life force from his servants.

The innkeeper then decided to listen to the words of the magician. He found a simple shepherd who was very humble, pure in heart and well-read. He brought the shepherd into his room and mixed the elements.

The shepherd saw nothing wrong with creating others like self, for he saw self to be good. He spoke the sacred words and breathed life into the bodies. Beautiful beings were manifested. They were pure in heart and wise and they loved self and life in all forms. They were brilliant. The innkeeper was proud. He loved his creations, for they were love manifest.

What he did not take into account was the wisdom, honesty and integrity endowed in them through the shepherd. They had minds of their own, and they would gladly serve the innkeeper as long as his desires were for the good of all. They could not harm, mistreat or bring distress to any living thing. They saw the Father within all things, and they saw men as their brothers. If ever a desire of the innkeeper did not align with their truth, they simply smiled and refused to do his bidding. The love and acceptance of self allowed this, for it was in the mind of the shepherd. They were steadfast.

The innkeeper could not find it within self to learn from his creations. His need to control and his desire to reign supreme once again became the motivating factor for his behavior. He soon became enraged with his servants' refusal to obey his commands. He told them he was their creator and that they must obey him. If they did not, he would destroy them with the sacred words to withdraw the life force.

One stood forward and spoke to the innkeeper. He said, "We are not of man, we are of spirit. From this we draw our sustenance. Though we love you and truly desire to serve, we cannot go against that which is instilled within us by the shepherd. We see that in your refusal to learn and change, it is necessary for us to leave this valley. We love you dearly, and we will create a kingdom that is beyond your dreams. This will be yours, if and only if, you can lay aside this need for control. You have taken a throne, but you are not fit to govern. The throne we shall give you is one earned by deeds. We have shown you the way. When you can lay aside your iniquities and become one with us, the throne will be yours. One day you will see that the throne is within the individual, along with the kingdom, and that the only reign is over oneself."

They banded together and left for the mountains with nothing, for they knew that which was within them would furnish all their needs. The innkeeper was enraged. He told them they would pay for their disobedience. He yelled, "You will be thrown into a pit of darkness where you will gnash your teeth and beg for mercy."

He then ran for the book. The shepherd met him at the door, book in hand. He said calmly, "These are my creations and sons unto me. What I have created shall not be put asunder. This book shall become their guide, for they are pure of heart."

The truth spoken forth caused the innkeeper to fall to the ground, kicking and screaming like a child. His prophecy had come true, for he was thrown into his own pit of darkness, where he lay gnashing his teeth. He paused for a moment, with an evil look in his eye. He stood erect, smiled and spoke, "I remember the words to withdraw the life force. I shall have my revenge." He screamed the words, with the force and conviction of a madman.

He then dropped dead. He had not read chapter four, where it was written, "... That which you speak and embrace emotionally, comes back to the source."

The shepherd joined his band, for they were left untouched. The belief instilled within them was that they were children of God and that to God they owed their allegiance and from God they drew their sustenance and protection. This was their reality. Thus, as you believe, so it is.

5

When You Call Upon the Light

Understandings, Tools & Techniques

When you call upon the light, a fire comes with it, and that fire evokes change. It is a fire of transmutation that amplifies and calls forward all that is of a lower vibration. The fire moves through your mental and emotional bodies, dissolving lower vibrational attitudes and emotions, as well as any limiting mental concepts, bringing you forward into a greater truth, a greater reality, a higher vibration.

Many of your fears, judgments, jealousies, angers and preconceived "isms," schisms and dogmatic teachings will be dissolved by the grace of the light. In some cases, you are not yet ready to let go of a past experience and the attitudes, emotions and wrong conclusions concerning the experience. Because you are holding them in your auric field, you manifest these experiences and magnetize events and people to share the experiences. You are all co-creating together. The light quickens experiences, manifesting them in your outer world, thus giving you the opportunity and understanding to heal any lower vibrational attitudes and emotions.

This also pertains to wrong conclusions from past experience. These manifestations are your teachers. They are gifts sent on the wings of love, and it is best that you learn from them and release and heal what is necessary. You cannot hide from your consciousness, and consciousness creates reality. You can postpone your healing, denying the experience and the teacher, and you can blame others, yet this will only set you up for grander teachers in the future.

We have not completely addressed your physical reality, which includes your physical body. Your body is a marvelous vehicle. Properly attuned, it can sense energies millions of miles away. It can sense the presence of high and low vibrations, and entities in this dimension or another. It can tell you exactly what you are dealing with on all levels. There are sensitives, or adepts, who can feel psychic bonds, thought forms and limiting mental concepts, as well as the presence of the Beautiful Many Ascended Ones, all with body signals. Pains and twitches, goose bumps, chills, feelings and sensations in the chakras or energy centers of the body all can tell you something. Some are messages that a healing is in order; some are calling cards of masters and guides. All in all, we strongly suggest listening to your body. It will talk to you.

The next understanding concerns the vibrational lifting of the body. The body is a physical manifestation of your mental and emotional body. It also carries with it cellular memory-the attitudes and emotions of your forefathers. Your body merely consists of coagulated thought, yours and theirs.

Denser, crystallized thought is dissolving and breaking up due to the vibrational lifting of this plane. It is released as toxins within the body. Your elimination systems are going to be on overload, collecting and eliminating these toxins. At times you will feel lethargic and tired, and need to process by laying down the body. At times this process may make you ill, or bring discomfort to a part of your body. In rare cases, you may think you are checking out, so to speak. In most cases, these experiences go as quickly as they come and in their passing you will feel more alive and healthy, with a change in attitude.

The last topic concerns help. You are not alone in this endeavor. There are brothers and sisters, seen and unseen, ministering to the needs of humanity. Some of you are receiving transmissions of love and power, healings and guidance from the Beautiful Many Ascended Ones. Many of you are experiencing an opening of the inner ear, along with ringing in your ears. This is your brethren trying to contact you. It is also opening you to higher frequency communication or higher vibrational thought. Ideas and feelings that accompany the ringing are gifts from on high. Vibrational liftings can space you out or cause your body to heat up, rock, shake or experience chills and goose bumps. Many will experience pressure, or a sensation on the crown of the head, as it opens to the new consciousness and energy. You are all unique, and the way you react to these energies will also be unique.

All in all, when you call upon the light, you call upon the fire. Have the courage and love of self to walk through the fire. What is waiting on the other side is a healthier, happier, more expanded you with greater love, joy and freedom. And when you hear a ringing in your ear, fill yourself with love, joy and gratitude for the Beautiful Many Ascended Ones, and know that you are not alone. Listen to them. Remember the greatest masters of all time were the greatest listeners. They found the time to go within and find self, for they were driven to do so, and they wanted to do so. Thus they gained their Christhood.

Commitment, Desire & Dedication

Let us begin with desire. Desire is the key that opens all doors. You cannot make the necessary commitment unless the desire is present. The commitment is relative to the desire. You cannot force yourself, for that diminishes your joy. When one truly desires something, he will commit to whatever is necessary to attain it. The degree of success is relative to the degree of commitment. If you truly desire oneness with spirit, it takes strong commitment and dedication to meditation.

It is written: "Be still and know ye are God." Meditation allows this. It dissolves all that which separates you from the one mind that is God. It dissolves all fear, unworthiness, false beliefs and the attitudes and emotions that conflict with the truth of your being. Pure, unconditional love and joy resides within you. It is the truth of your being, and meditation allows you to access this truth.

It is also written: "The light that dwells within all men is the light of God." Calling this light forward and becoming one with it creates union. This union is called the Christ, Emmanuel, or God within us. In reality, you are only a channel for God. For God to work through you, there must be a clearing away of all that is out of alignment with the mind of God. Meditation assists you in doing this. As spirit flows through you, it will clear away that which is out of alignment.

You all have unique talents and abilities. The Christ energy enhances them. It enhances your creativity, your love, your joy, your wisdom, your health and your life in general. I cannot expound enough on the benefits of meditation. Meditation can be used for inner guidance, or for directing energy and healing to a place in need. There are guided meditations and meditations for guidance. We will give you a little of both to assist you in your awakening.

In all meditation, begin by surrounding yourself with light, either gold or white. Have your chosen representative of the Father assist you. If something doesn't feel right, heal until you feel clear. We will give a method of healing that will assist you.

There is one precaution. Venturing into new territory creates a greater need for self-authority and healing. As you expand in consciousness and become more sensitive, the ability to heal what is within that greater reality is of utmost importance.

You will only expand to the extent that you feel safe and free of negative influences. Enjoy the love, joy, wisdom and power and, by all means, use the tools. Allow nothing to stand between you and the unique loving, joyous, powerful, manifesting God that you are. It is your birthright.

There is one more topic we would like to address. Do not try to blank out your mind. Your mind is a computer that is constantly in action. Let it run. Do not fight it. Allow it, and shift into higher frequency thought. Focus on love and joy and feel yourself expanding. In time, your mind will run out of gas, so to speak, the chattering will ease up, and higher frequency attitudes and emotions of higher consciousness will begin to take over. Continue to fill yourself with love and joy, and you will ascend in consciousness. What you are looking for are levels of higher frequency thought-interdimensional mind. If you try to stop the mind, you will set yourself up for failure. If a lower vibrational attitude or emotion comes forward, simply heal it with a corresponding principle or truth. Release it and move on.

Channeling

All of your sacred books speak of channeling in one form or another. What do you think prophecy is? All of your saints and sages were channels. They were all unique expressions of God. When Jesus spoke the words, "I of myself do nothing, it is the Father within that doeth the works," he was explaining a method of allowing the Father to flow through him in all of his words and deeds. Paul said that we have "bodies terrestrial and bodies celestial." He was explaining our celestial counterparts-aspects of self expressing on other planes and dimensions.

You all have guides, angels and celestial counterparts to assist you. If it is your will, they will bring more love and joy into your life. They will also bring more unlimited thought, which assists you in more unlimited creations. You must expand your reality beyond the physical body and the intellect. You have allowed fear and false beliefs to separate you from the rest of the universe. Not one of you is unworthy of channeling the "All That Is The All" into all that you say and do. This was the message Jesus conveyed when he spoke the words, "Ye will do greater works than I, for I go on to the Father."

We must go back to your origin to truly understand channeling. In the beginning, you were given consciousness and free will. The consciousness was the same consciousness as God. This was the understanding conveyed by Jesus when he said, "Ye are all Gods." It is also written that you were created in the same image and likeness of God. This being your true nature, it is perfectly logical that in consciousness, you are one with all life and can connect with any life form you choose. In reality, you are light beings expressing in a physical body, and when you recognize this, you are unlimited. You are also connected to the whole of life no matter where it is expressing-another plane, another dimension, even the plants and animals in this dimension. The consciousness in which all things reside is the mind of God. It is your true nature, your true consciousness, the consciousness of your origin. Many call channeling a phenomenon. I call it remembering.

There are a few guidelines to pure and safe channeling. One of the most important things to remember is:

Messages are only as clear as the entity or level one has attuned to. They are also only as clear as the channel delivering the message.

If you are receiving a channeled message, you are responsible for discerning whether that message is true for you. Go within and trust your feelings. The channel is responsible for his or her own clarity and tuning. A good channel delivers around seventy percent of the message clearly and accurately. The rest of the message is subject to interference or the channel's own preconceived ideas or limiting mental concepts.

You can check the accuracy of your channeling. Humbly ask the masters to show you a dial from one to one hundred. Then have them show you a mark on the dial that indicates the percentage of clear and accurate channeling. As you practice, the percentage will increase. There are times, however, when you cross a new threshold that your usual percentage may drop. Continue to practice, and soon you will be channeling messages from the highest vibration.

If you receive messages of hierarchies, with lords that dispense justice and control your destiny, then self-authority and discernment are in order. These ideas don't correspond to the image of God in which you were created, or to the divine right to free will. If you feel the presence of a lower vibration, be it an entity or attitude or emotion, go to the next section, "Healing Lower Vibrational Influences" and heal until it feels clear.

For your next understanding, I would like to remind you of unconditional love. Do not take it upon yourself to judge and condemn those who are not as clear as you are. If it feels right, teach them how to heal and attune to higher levels. Those who are beginning to channel often tend to color messages or connect with the first entity that comes to them. A good thing to remember is: just because a person is dead, it doesn't follow that he is enlightened. Again, if you are experiencing lower vibrational attitudes, emotions, thought forms, limiting mental concepts or discarnate spirits that feel negative, follow the steps given in the section on healing negative influences.

Clear channels clear their space before expanding and opening to higher vibrations. They also keep it clear. This insures truth of the highest vibration and lifts and heals those who come to experience the channel. Unconditional love, joy and freedom are the best tools for discernment. It is unwise to be skeptical, just as it is unwise to be gullible. Open yourself to a greater reality, and feel whether the information expands and empowers you. Presently, there is a lot of channeled information coming in through books and gatherings. As time moves forward, that which is true will stand on its own merit. That which is false will fall away. It is the nature of truth.

Healing Lower Vibrational Influences

Many unseen influences affect your daily lives. Most of these influences are positive, yet some are of a lower vibrational nature. There are lower vibrational discarnate spirits, thought forms, limiting mental concepts and psychic bonds.

Discarnate spirits of lower vibrational nature are lost souls. They are people who, upon their transition (some call it death), have remained on the Earth vibration. They are in between worlds due to strong bonds with loved ones, unfinished business, or a sudden or a seemingly untimely death. Although they are no longer physical, they continue in an astral body that has within it a mental and emotional body. Poltergeists fall into this category. They are usually mischievous children who have also made their transition. Those who are incarnate ("in the physical") also have mental and emotional bodies and can be affected by the attitudes and emotions of lower vibrational discarnate spirits. Excessive guilt, anger, sickness, confusion, multiple accidents and suicidal tendencies can all be by-products of an extreme degree of influence or possession.

Psychic bonds can be with either incarnate or discarnate beings. These are connections through which lower vibrational attitudes and emotions travel.

Limiting mental concepts and thought forms can also inhibit your greater good. Limiting mental concepts are false beliefs in sickness, lack, or anything that limits you from living a loving, joyous, abundant life. Thought forms are demons, monsters and other forms generated in the mind. They consist of coagulated thought. Many psychedelic experiences are thought forms. Lower vibrational influences can make you both mentally and physically ill.

These influences are not bound by time, distance or space. They exist in the mental realm, which is a blessing, because all that exists in the mental realm can be healed within the mind.

You have a protective light, or aura, around your body that shields you from most lower vibrational influences. All lower vibrational influences can be easily healed, and it is our desire to give you some power tools to do so.

We are using the words "power tools" because it best describes what is being given. A tool does not work by itself. It is something to assist in bringing about a desired effect. A power tool must be plugged in.

Likewise, one must plug in, so to speak, to the power within to use these tools. It is important to know that those you are healing are the ones in trouble. Know that you are safe and protected. By all means, stay out of fear. Healings are to be done in love, for love is the ultimate power in the universe. It is the source, and the more you become one with love and joy, the more powerful your healings become.

It is also wise never to judge yourself, or fear you did not do the healing properly, or say the words in the right order, or deem yourself unworthy of such a momentous task. What you are doing is a simple healing in conjunction with a Christed master who is very allowing, forgiving and patient, and who loves you unconditionally. Your intent is known and the master's joy and admiration for any effort on your part is overwhelming. They will fill in any gaps and see that the healing is complete in the beginning. Just keep practicing, and soon you will become proficient. As you work by yourself or with others, you will soon see results that will help you gain a conviction.

It may be disquieting to learn that all that "stuff" is out there. Yet you have been living in it all the time. Nothing has really changed now, has it? The only thing changed is that instead of being a victim of lower vibrational influences, you can have dominion over them, if you use the tools for healing. That is what it is all about: lifting and empowering the individual. You have within you the most powerful tool in the universe. It is called mind. It can direct the full power of God into any situation you desire. That power is love.

Monitor yourself, honor your feelings; and if you don't like what you are feeling, do a healing. We will be with you, within you, all the way. Your help is greatly needed and appreciated, for there is not only work to do upon this plane, where you reside, but on other planes as well. A ground crew is of the utmost importance in the healing and vibrational lifting of the planet. There are many, incarnate and discarnate, that need physical examples of the light on the Earth. That is where their attention is focused and that is where they can best receive healing. This will answer that age-old question, "Why me?

With all the great, omnipresent masters, why me?" It is because you are a master as well, residing in the physical. It is in the physical that you have a chance to demonstrate-sometimes against all odds. That is why you are a master: You have all it takes.

Healing Negative Influences

Healing is a must for all those who desire to operate in other realms of consciousness. You must have self-authority and maintain control. If you are experiencing negative vibrations, they are either thought forms, limiting mental concepts, psychic bonds or discarnate entities (lost souls) in need of healing. They are bound to the Earth vibration due to lower vibrational attitudes and emotions. Some are coercive and desire to manipulate and control. Love heals. Casting out only sends them to another place, another person. In all healing, remember that God is love. It is the power of love that heals and lifts. We will give you the following steps to clear the energy.

1. Close your aura by visualizing a white or gold light around you.
2. Call upon your chosen cultural representative of God, be it Jesus, Buddha, Babaji, Mary, Mohammed, White Eagle or another one of the Beautiful Many Christed Ones.
3. Tell the entities they are healed and forgiven, lifted and enlightened.
4. Tell them they are filled and surrounded with the Christ light and the Christ love.
5. Ask your chosen representative to take them to their perfect place.
6. Ask that all negative thought forms and limiting mental concepts be dissolved and lifted in the light of truth.
7. Ask that all psychic bonds be severed, and close their auras to all but spirit of the highest vibration.

Repeat this process until you feel clear. There may be more than one healing to do. Remember your word is very powerful, and what is spoken on their level manifests instantly. Many enlightened ones use this process before opening. It creates a clear and safe environment, and it also lifts the one who is doing the healing. Intent is nine-tenths of the law. If you intend to serve and heal, you will draw to you entities of like mind. If you intend to coerce or manipulate, again, you will draw entities of like mind. It is the law of attraction.

At times, discarnate spirits will come to your light like a moth to a flame. Do not judge yourself, simply heal them. They are the ones in trouble, not you. They are seeking your help.

Advanced Healing

As you become more proficient in healing and can attune to higher levels, thereby generating more power, you may be called on to heal numerous possessing entities and levels of discarnate spirits (upon which there may be hundreds). This may also include lost souls that are alien in nature. After all, humanity is not the only civilization that experiences death. Discarnate spirits that are alien in nature often call for greater self authority on your part. They can be a little stubborn. Do not get into fear. Your Christ self, or any Christed master, can handle any situation and has the means to call forward all the help that is necessary.

There exist pockets where souls of like mind, seen and unseen, gather. As you contact, or pass through these areas, it is possible to feel the pain, sadness, sorrow and even the sickness in the minds of souls on the physical and astral levels. It can cause pain, nausea, headaches, etc. It can be overwhelming at times.

When you experience this, claim to yourself, "Not mine!" Even if you think it's yours, it is not the truth of your being. Claim protection. Close your aura to all but the Christ energy and acknowledge that you are a unique, loving, joyous, whole and healthy, eternal God endowed with the divine right to choose your reality. Whatever you focus on becomes your reality.

Once you are centered in the truth of your being, heal all that is of a lower vibrational nature-all that you feel. Claim your true identity with self-authority. Remain steadfast, and allow the Christ within to flow through you and heal until it feels clear again.

When healing multiple possessions on levels, follow the same format, yet know that you are speaking to each possessing entity and to all influencing entities on all levels. This directs the healing energies to each and every one of them. It is not necessary to know, on an intellectual level, how many there are. The Christed masters working through you will direct the energy where it is needed. As you become more sensitive you will be able to discern the numbers.

There are psychokinetic tools that can help you. Some use tables to tip out the numbers of entities, some use body signals, some use divining rods and some use pendulums. Whatever you use, make sure it is orchestrated by, and that you are attuned to, a Christed master or what is known as the Christ vibration.

If the advanced healing is a little too far out for you, put it on the shelf and begin with the first techniques given. Allow yourself to unfold gracefully. Stay in control, keep your self-authority, and attune to the highest level of pure unconditional love. This is where the power to heal comes from.

There will come a time when healings will be no longer necessary, when all lower vibrational influences will have been healed and lifted in the light on all planes and dimensions throughout the universe. Until that day comes, there is a lot of work to do "together."

Om Circles & Toning

Om is actually spelled "aum." It represents three aspects of God: Creation, Preservation and Destruction. These are aspects, or cycles, of nature. Aum is a tone, or vibration, that will, with the proper intent, open doorways to Spirit. It can be used for sending love, joy or healing. It can also be used to receive the same blessings. Contrary to the belief of many, it is not a tool of the devil. When done properly, it sounds surprisingly familiar to "amen," which, in truth, owes its ancient roots to its beginning as aum. We will give you a few examples.

First set the intent as follows:

Aum receive-The love and joy of God. (This should be repeated by the group.) Now in unison do the aum.

Aum send-The healing light of God. (This should be repeated by the group.) Again, in unison, do the aum.

If it feels better to say amen, by all means do so. Intent is the law. If you intend to send or receive the light, it will happen.

Be creative with this, and remember that thought is the cause. Sending a healing thought to a friend or putting yourself in a state of receivership for a loving, joyous or healing thought is truly a blessing. When received, the thought will lift and heal. It is that simple. You can also use the aum circle for world healing. Set the intent and aum.

Toning is similar to the aum. Following the same technique, use the word in a long drawn out tone. The only difference is that we use the vowels (A E I O U).

You are all known throughout the universe as a combination of tones. You have a Soul tone, a Christ tone and an "I am" tone, as well as a few tones in between. Each level is a combination of tones, and when they all come together, it creates a beautiful symphony.

Toning helps one to balance the body and clear any lower vibrations. It can be used to clear a room, or like the Aborigines use it, to clear a whole valley. Play with them and feel which ones are right for you.

The Golden Wheel - A Group Meditation

Begin with a candle; the more the merrier. Place it at the center of the room. Form a circle around the candle. Take a few moments to center, and visualize yourself in a bubble of light. Now create a bubble collectively around the group. If you feel any negative vibrations, heal them with the techniques mentioned in an earlier section until it feels clear.

Start by visualizing a golden ball in the center of the group. See it spinning counterclockwise. See a spoke come from the center straight into your heart. Know this is the love and joy of the Father.

Visualize another ball of golden light coming in on your left and moving out on your right. See it moving faster and faster. Visualize a wheel with the hub in the center of the room, the spokes spinning and the ball moving through the group like the rim of the wheel. See this wheel spinning faster and faster, and, as it spins, feel yourself expanding, lifting into a higher vibration. See it spinning faster and faster, lifting the entire room.

Feel yourself expanding and lifting into the higher vibrations of love and joy. Stay as long as the energy holds.

When you feel it is time, come back into an objective state.

Feel this energy moving into the Earth, grounding it into the physical. You will find yourself elevated to a higher state of consc10usness.

World Healing

The wheel exercise in a group meditation is a good one for world healings. After you have lifted the group and established the energy, visualize a crystalline tube going from the center of your group to the area of the world you desire to treat. Send the golden ball of energy you generated to the location you desire, through the tube. Visualize it blazing through the area, dissolving all lower vibrational attitudes and emotions. See it anchor the love and joy of its vibration in the area. Know that it is a forever light that will continue in its healing and lifting.

It is wise to heal any discarnate spirits, limiting mental concepts, thought forms and psychic bonds affecting any of the principal players in world situations.

Another spin-off of this exercise is to put the Earth in the center of the room and use the golden ball, spinning and swirling, to cleanse and lift the entire planet. Use violet, blue, green, pink, gold or white light, which has all the colors within it. Each color carries with it a healing vibration.

1.   Violet-Transmutation
2.   Blue-Love and Wisdom
3.   Green-Healing
4.   Pink-Love
5.   Gold-Joy

These meditations are for the purpose of opening and guiding the mind to realization of the desired effect. They assist you in gaining conviction. They help focus the mind. In groups, these meditations create a unified focus. The power of a loving, joyous, healing thought, generated collectively, invokes great change.

There will come a time when these exercises are no longer necessary. You will have the conviction and focus necessary to create the desired effect without all the steps. After all, isn't that what this is all about?

Opening to Spirit

1.   Begin by sitting comfortably in a chair or on the floor. Visualize yourself and the room filled with light. Close your aura to all but spirit and see yourself surrounded by the white light of the Christ vibration.

2.   Call upon your representative of the Father to assist you, or ask the Father to assist you.

3.   Visualize a white or golden light spinning and swirling at the crown of your head.

4.   Move this light down to your third eye (located at the center of your forehead, just above and between your eyes). Spin and swirl the light through this area. Visualize it clearing this chakra.

5.   Move it downward to the throat chakra, repeating the process.

6. Move it downward to the next chakra (the heart), again spinning and swirling the light.

7. Move it downward to the solar plexus. Spinning, swirling and clearing.

8. Then downward to the area just below the navel.

9. Finally, move it to the root chakra, at the base of the spine.

10. Now take this light energy and create an anchor into the Earth. This will help ground you.

11. Now, visualize a crystalline tube that is impenetrable. Visualize this tube rising from you and attaching to the from the Godhead. Feel it click into place. Know that nothing can enter this tube but spirit of the highest vibration.

12. Run the golden ball from the base of your spine upwards to the Godhead.

13. Now, feel the pure love and joy of spirit descending into your body, filling you with Grace.

14. You have created a clear path of golden energy upon which spirit can travel.

15. Practice this daily and soon you will be a clear receiver for spirit in all that you say and do.

Many have received miraculous healings, powerful love feelings and vibrational liftings using this exercise.

Greeting the Sun

To those early risers, I give a technique that will allow you to move rapidly in your spiritual growth.

1. Begin your day with a few stretches and exercises-Yoga, Tai Chi, whatever feels good.

2. Sit facing the East. If you are up early enough, you can greet

the sun as it rises. Do not worry if you are a little late. Just close your eyes and turn toward the sun-facing the sun is the issue.

3. Give thanks to the sun. See it as the source of all that is-the light where everything began. Allow this light to blaze through your being, fortifying your aura.

4. Feel the rays of love and joy warming you, lifting you, permeating every cell. See it dissolving any darkness, lighting up your physical body, your emotional body and your mental body.

5. See the sun as your spiritual body coming forward, lifting and healing, until your entire being is pulsating and glowing with the love and joy of spirit.

6. Carry with you the idea of the sun that shines on everything evenly, loving all creation unconditionally.

This will greatly enhance your day. It will energize you, heal you, and open you, to greater understanding.

Prayers of the Masters

These prayers we give you are truly powerful tools if spoken with conviction and if recited during meditation. If you can, find a quiet, unspoiled spot in nature where you will not be distracted, judged or interrupted by the thoughts and emotions of others. If you cannot take the time to be in a place such as this, do the best you can with what you have.

How to Pray for Guidance

Within each and every one of us resides a unique, loving, joyous, wise and powerful manifesting God, born of the original light from which nothing is withheld. These prayers for guidance and manifestation are invoking and calling forward this original light. The degree of success is directly related to your consciousness and your conviction.

The original light you are evoking must pass through layers of fear, unworthiness, confusion, doubt and wrong conclusions from past experiences held within your consciousness. The more you practice evoking this original light, the clearer you become. As direct knowing and manifestation begins to occur, it will help you to gain a conviction.

Do not sabotage your effort by choosing something beyond your ability to accept, or trespass upon another god's divine right to free will and self-determination.

Pray for the highest and best good for all concerned-that each person find their perfect place. Start out with something you can believe in or accept.

Embrace each desire emotionally. Live it as a fantasy, as if it were already manifested.

Build a conviction as each manifestation takes shape, and always allow love to be the manifesting force behind all creation. We will help you until you remember.

Prayer for Guidance & Manifestation

Prayer for Guidance
>
> Beloved Father, Mother, God
> That which is all-knowing
> That which is within
> That which I am
> Come forth, come forth, come forth
> Come forth in love, joy, wisdom and power
> Dissolve the clouds of fear, confusion and misperception
> I am, I know, guide me this hour.

Prayer for Manifestation
>
> Beloved Father, Mother, God
> That which is within
> That which I am
> Come forth, come forth, come forth
> Come forth into power
> Fulfill this desire
> To the glory of God
> To the power within
> So will it manifest
> Thank you
> I release it now!

These prayers are not set in stone. You can make up your own and alter them. Use whatever words feel right. That's what creativity is all about. Have fun. Don't make a somber ritual about it. It is through joy that the word manifests.

Simple Truths To Get You By

The Father Mother God principle, known as life, is one consciousness that encompasses all consciousness. It is omnipresent on all planes and all dimensions throughout the universe. It is all that is. Wherever there is life, there is God.

Consciousness creates reality. People and events are magnetized to and manifested in your daily lives according to your consciousness. The destiny of the world is created by the individual and collective consciousness of those who reside upon it. You are living in an action-reaction world known as the plane of demonstration, where consciousness creates reality. Renew the mind, renew the world.

Your physical body is an expression of your mental and emotional bodies. It is endowed with your attitudes and emotions, along with those you genetically inherited from your forefathers. We are telling you this so that you won't be so hard on yourself when your body runs amuck.

The God within you has the power to heal both your hang-ups and your forefathers' hang-ups, bringing you into the whole and healthy now.

God, humanity and nature are one. No matter how hard you try, you cannot separate yourself, humanity in all its diversity, and nature from omnipresence. You can only live the illusion.

Love God with all your heart. Honor each individual as a unique expression of God, and behave as if the God in all life matters. If you want to experience Heaven on Earth, start treating Earth like Heaven.

There, you are enlightened. Now, go out and do something with it! Be a blessing to life.

Your Beloved Brother,
Cazekiel

Conclusion

These truths that have been given you are not for everyone. Not everyone is ready for such outrageous wisdom. Many will cling to the recycled ignorance of social consciousness. Others will cling to their religious dogma or scientific dogma. Some seemingly cannot afford to accept this truth. They will cling to their positions, jobs, material acquisitions and money-those things that are "real." (A little cosmic humor there ....)

What has been given is what is real. All will make itself known in your very near future. The days of ignorance are coming to a close, along with the reign of those who have kept you in darkness. The reign of those whose empires were built at the expense of humanity and nature are also coming to a close. The Earth changes will become very real. They are already upon you and will escalate in the future. The days of denial, too, are coming to a close. The enlightened masters upon this plane are screaming at humanity to get your act together and stop your self-destructive behavior. Even those you know as Archangels are very concerned and are delivering the same message. Due to denial and vested interest, many ignore this message, and some even deem it unspiritual. The enlightened ones are all telling you this because they love you. They want to get you through an age.

I am one of these beloved brothers who also loves you greatly and cares deeply for each and every one of you. We also cherish a planet called Earth more than you know. We hold all life as sacred. Even you, despite what you think of yourselves or what you have done, are greatly loved. We have brought this message to other civilizations in the past, the remnants of which are you. We have incarnated upon this plane so humanity could hear this same message. It was delivered by Buddha, Mohammed, Jesus, White Eagle, Mary and a host of other masters, saints and sages, only to be organized and altered by kings and institutions.

We have told you to love God, the omnipresent life force, with all your heart. We told you to love your neighbor, which is humanity with all of its diverse cultures and beliefs. We have also told you to cherish all life as sacred, for where there is life, there is God. These three simple truths, if honored with impeccable integrity, will solve all the ills of humanity.

The greatest teaching of all time is that "Ye are Gods." If that is all that is accomplished in these writings, we have done our work. As mentioned before, no matter how hard you try, you cannot separate yourself, humanity in all its diversity, and nature from the omnipresent life force known as God. Let love be the manifesting force behind all creation, and behave as if the God in all life matters. Be a blessing to life.

I am Cazekiel,
God of Eternal Bliss.
I love you greatly.

About the Author

James Gilliland is a minister, counselor, an internationally known lecturer, best selling author with the books, Reunion with Source, Becoming Gods, and The Ultimate Soul Journey. James appeared in Contact Has Begun, His Story, The History Channel, UFOs then and Now, UFO Hotspots, ABC, Fox News, BBC Danny Dyer Special, Paranormal State, ECETI Ranch a Documentary, and the new movie Thrive have all featured James and ECETI which he is the founder.

He has appeared on Coast to Coast, Jeff Rense, and to numerous other radio shows to mention also being the host of, As You Wish Talk Radio, www.bbsradio.com and Contact Has Begun, www.worldpuja.net. He is a facilitator of many Eastern disciplines, a visionary dedicated to the awakening and healing of Humanity and the Earth and teaches higher dimensional realities from experience.

For other books by James, DVD's, conferences, updates and more go to www.eceti.org

Last Prayer

Beloved Father, do you think they understood the true meaning of my message, my life? That Ye are all Gods. That Ye will do greater works than I for I am leaving this plane. Do you think they understood my prayer when I said Beloved Father let them be one as we are one, that within them resides a loving, joyous, wise and powerful manifesting God waiting to unfold? Do you think they understood the true meaning of my death and my resurrection which was to conquer the greatest of all challenges and fears which is death itself? Do you think they understood unconditional love, infinite compassion and forgiveness? Will it take another 2,000 years of fear, unworthiness, separation, the worshipping and warring over names, images and doctrines before they find peace, unity and the God within them? Will they ever understand the one law which supersedes all laws which is the law of love?

A Message from Mother Mary

In the days to come it is imperative that each individual establish his or her own God connection, his or her own inner guidance and act upon it without attachment or denial. They will be the seed people after the changes for the Golden Age of God.